Commercial Landowner
CERCLA Liability Protection

Understanding the Final EPA "All Appropriate Inquiries" Rule and Revised ASTM Phase I

Barry A. Cik

Government Institutes
An imprint of
The Scarecrow Press, Inc.
Lanham, Maryland • Toronto • Oxford
2006

Government Institutes

Published in the United States of America
by Government Institutes, an imprint of The Scarecrow Press, Inc.
A wholly owned subsidiary of
The Rowman & Littlefield Publishing Group, Inc.
4501 Forbes Boulevard, Suite 200
Lanham, Maryland 20706
http://www.govinstpress.com/

PO Box 317
Oxford
OX2 9RU, UK

British Library Cataloguing in Publication Information Available

Library of Congress Cataloging-in-Publication Data

Cik, Barry A., 1951–
  Commercial landowner CERCLA liability protection : understanding the final
EPA "All Appropriate Inquiries" Rule and revised ASTM Phase I / Barry A.
Cik.
    p. cm.
  ISBN-13: 978-0-86587-157-1 (pbk. : alk. paper)
  ISBN-10: 0-86587-157-4 (pbk. : alk. paper)
  1. Liability for environmental damages—United States. 2. Commercial real
estate—United States. I. Title.
  KF1298.Z9C55 2006
    344.7304'6—dc22   2006012440

The paper used in this publication meets the minimum requirements of
American National Standard for Information Sciences—Permanence of
Paper for Printed Library Materials, ANSI/NISO Z39.48-1992.
Manufactured in the United States of America.

In gratitude to

Regina Cik
David and Lisa Jilbert
Lisa and Antonio La Spina

Table of Contents

ABOUT BARRY A. CIK / G.E.M. TESTING & ENGINEERING LABS

Barry A. Cik: Barry A. Cik is a quarter century veteran in the environmental investigation and assessment of commercial and industrial properties. Mr. Cik focuses on: (a) environmental risk management/due diligence for buyers, sellers, lenders and owners; and (b) development of toxic-free and healthier consumer products that protect human health, safety and the environment.

Barry A. Cik is a
- BCEE—Board Certified Environmental Engineer [#98-20076],
  American Academy of Environmental Engineers
- PE—Licensed & Registered Professional Engineer [#47615],
  State of Ohio
- CP—Certified Professional [#109],
  State of Ohio EPA VAP
- QEP—Qualified Environmental Professional [#01960005],
  Institute of Professional Environmental Practice
- REM—Registered Environmental Manager [#05594],
  National Registry of Environmental Professionals
- CHMM—Certified Hazardous Materials Manager [#10795], Master Level,
  Institute of Hazardous Materials Management
- Certified Diplomate Forensic Engineer [#681]
  National Academy of Forensic Engineers

Barry A. Cik has been a member ASTM Committee E50 for most of its existence (since its founding in 1991). He currently serves on subcommittee E50.02, which has direct responsibility for the ASTM Phase I Standard Practice.

Barry A. Cik is Chief Engineer at G.E.M. Testing & Engineering Labs.
He can be reached at 216-781-4120; 216-381-3153; 216-288-0995; or barry@gemtesting.com.

G.E.M. Testing & Engineering Labs: G.E.M. Testing provides Phase I & II and other environmental due diligence services for chemical and industrial operations, commercial businesses, real estate investors/developers, lenders, attorneys and government entities.

G.E.M. Testing's project consulting services are designed to assist buyers, sellers, lenders and owners in finding optimal solutions for difficult environmental issues.

G.E.M. Testing & Engineering Labs provides professional services in all fifty states.
G.E.M. Testing can be reached at 1-888-9-GEM-TEST or www.gemtesting.com.

StarSafe™: StarSafe is a consulting and product development service affiliated with G.E.M. Testing & Engineering Labs designed to
(a) identify the unnecessary uses of toxic chemicals in consumer products;
(b) investigate the connections between toxic chemicals and the protection of human health, safety and the environment;
and (c) develop alternate consumer product formulations that minimize the use of unnecessary toxic chemicals.

StarSafe™ can be reached at 1-888-99-ENVIRO or www.gemtesting.com.

DISCLAIMERS

Summary Only: The information presented herein is intended as a summary only. It does not replace the actual AAI Final Rule or the ASTM Phase I Environmental Site Assessment.

General Information: The information presented is intended as general information for educational purposes. While believed to be generally accurate and reliable, it may contain errors or omissions and no representations are made regarding accuracy or applicability. Application or use of any information is at the user's sole risk.

Opinions of the Author Only: All interpretations and opinions are strictly that of the author. No implication is intended that U.S. EPA, ASTM International, or any other entity approves or endorses the contents of this book or any portions thereof. The reader is encouraged to obtain the complete original documents.

No Legal Advice: The information presented does not replace the need for competent legal advice. In particular, the application of any information to the circumstances of any particular property or situation should only be done under the direction and advice of a qualified attorney.

Corrections Appreciated: Any recommendations or corrections may be relayed to the author and will be appreciated: Barry A. Cik 216-781-4120; 216-381-3153; or barry@gemtesting.com

INTRODUCTION

The U.S. EPA "All Appropriate Inquiries" (AAI) Final Rule (released on November 1, 2005) significantly changes the manner in which environmental site assessments are performed for real estate properties. The ASTM Phase I Standard Practice, hitherto the most accepted guide to "All Appropriate Inquiries," has been revised to be consistent with the U.S. EPA AAI Final Rule and has been approved by the U.S. EPA.

AAI provides property owners with two new landowner liability protections in addition to the well-known Innocent Landowner (Innocent Purchaser) defense. The additional protections include the Contiguous Property Owner and the Bona Fide Prospective Purchaser liability protections.

The Bona Fide Prospective Purchaser protection is particularly noteworthy in that it provides liability protection to property owners regarding known contamination on their properties, provided that "All Appropriate Inquiries" was done prior to acquisition and which demonstrated that all contamination occurred prior to acquisition. However, prospective landowners (buyers) must recognize that even with the landowner liability protections, they may still have various Continuing Obligations regarding any hazardous substances at the property.

The AAI landowner liability protections encourage redevelopment of older industrial "Brownfields" properties, being that new owners of such properties can now be substantially protected against cleanup liability. AAI also provides an incentive for prospective landowners of commercial/ industrial properties "to know" and document any contamination prior to acquisition.

AAI sets minimum qualifications for Environmental Professionals (EP) and then relies on the professional judgment of the Environmental Professional. Environmental Professionals must provide opinions regarding conditions indicative of releases or threatened releases of hazardous substances and address data gaps.

Site assessments continue to require government records searches, historical research, inspections and interviews, as has been the case with the prior ASTM Phase I protocol. However, new protocols are included in AAI. These include the requirements to review local government records, institutional and engineering controls and environmental cleanup liens. AAI also emphasizes the importance of historical research, including the requirement that historical searches go back to the "first developed use" of the property.

Neither AAI nor ASTM require Phase II sampling and analysis in order to get any of the property owner liability protections. However, AAI suggests that this may be appropriate in some cases. In particular, sampling and analysis may be helpful in confirming that contamination in fact occurred prior to acquisition (thereby assisting with the Bona Fide Prospective Purchaser protection), and/or to help explain data gaps.

AAI allows prospective landowners "a way to get out of CERLCA environmental liability." However, this benefit comes with a co-requisite acceptance on the part of the prospective landowner to comply with Continuing Obligations, prevent any further environmental degradation of the property and protect human health, safety and the environment.

PART I: "ALL APPROPRIATE INQUIRIES" BASICS

A. Introduction

1. **General Objective:** This guide is intended to highlight the salient points of the U.S. EPA "All Appropriate Inquiries" (AAI) Final Rule and the revised ASTM Phase I Environmental Site Assessment Standard Practice (ASTM E1527-05). The perspective is to assist prospective landowners (buyers) or U.S. EPA Grantees to achieve the various landowner liability protections available under the "Brownfields Amendments."

    Included in the objective is addressing the interrelationships between these two documents, and, as appropriate, contrasts with the prior ASTM Phase I.

2. **Relevant AAI & ASTM Documents:** This guide is based on (U.S.) EPA 40 CFR Part 312, Standards and Practices for All Appropriate Inquiries; Final Rule, November 1, 2005; and ASTM E1527-05, Standard Practice for Environmental Site Assessments: Phase I Environmental Site Assessment Process.

    The AAI Final Rule was released by U.S. EPA on November 1, 2005 and comes after an earlier release of the Proposed Rule on August 26, 2004. The Proposed Rule was developed using a negotiated rulemaking process which included the participation of a diverse representation of affected parties. Additionally, subsequent to release of the Proposed Rule, the U.S. EPA reviewed over 400 public comments prior to development of the Final Rule.
    The ASTM E1527-05 (the revised Phase I) was approved in 2005 and released November 18, 2005. It is distinct from earlier ASTM Phase I Standard Practices (ASTM E1527-93, E1527-97 and E1527-00). The E1527 Phase I Standard Practice is under the jurisdiction of ASTM committee E50 on Environmental Assessments and is the specific responsibility of subcommittee E50.02 on Commercial Real Estate Transactions.

3. **Effective Dates:** The U.S. EPA AAI Final Rule was signed on November 1, 2005. It goes into effect on November 1, 2006. (Its use before that date is optional.)

    The revised ASTM Phase I was published November 18, 2005 and was effective immediately (although the AAI Final Rule recognizes the use of the prior ASTM Phase I until November 1, 2006).

    Note that even though the Final Rule goes into effect on November 1, 2006, "All Appropriate Inquiries" liability protections went into effect as of January 11, 2002, when the Brownfields Amendments was signed. (See FF: Interim Standards.)

4. **Basic Terminology:**
    a. "All Appropriate Inquiries" is also known simply as AAI.
        "All Appropriate Inquiries" and "All Appropriate Inquiry" are used interchangeably.
        (U.S. EPA tends to use the former and ASTM tends to use the latter.)
    b. "Brownfields Amendments," the "statute," and the "law" are used interchangeably.
    c. "AAI Final Rule," "U.S. EPA Final Rule," and "the rule" are used interchangeably.
    d. "Prior" ASTM Standard refers to the ASTM E1527-00 Standard Practice.
        "Revised" ASTM Standard refers to the ASTM E1527-05 Standard Practice.
        Note: The "00" or "05" at the end refers to the year when the ASTM Standard Practice was last revised.

5. **Focus of Presentation:** In general, the focus throughout this book is first on the AAI Final Rule, and second on ASTM and how it compliments AAI. In particular, ASTM Phase I requirements or guidance is usually specifically labeled as "ASTM."

6. **References:** References to the "AAI Final Rule" include the actual Final Rule as well as the Preamble (all of which is included in 40 CFR Part 312).

Note: <u>References to the Preamble of the AAI Final Rule do not have the same standing as the Final Rule itself, but, at a minimum, help explain the thinking and position of the U.S. EPA.</u>

The references in this document are generally given as "AAI Final Rule, Section __, pg __" or "Subpart __, § __, pg.__." The complete reference in each case would be (U.S.) EPA 40 CFR Part 312, Standards and Practices for All Appropriate Inquiries; Federal Register/Vol.70, No.210/Tuesday, November 1, 2005/Rules and Regulations; Final Rule; Section __, pg__ or Subpart __, § __, pg.__."

B. Regulatory Background

1. **CERCLA:** The Comprehensive Environmental Response, Compensation and Liability Act (42 U.S.C. § 9601), a.k.a. "CERCLA" or "Superfund" (1980), is the underlying federal statute for cleanup of historically contaminated properties. CERCLA introduced "strict, retroactive, joint and several liability" for property contaminated with CERCLA hazardous substances, whereby current owners of such contaminated properties can be potentially liable for their cleanup, even if the current owners were not themselves in any way involved in the contaminating actions. Liability is broad and includes owners, operators and generators.

   In effect, *if you buy the property, you buy the contamination.*

2. **SARA (Superfund Amendments):** The first revision was SARA (Public Law No. 99-499, 100 Stat. 1613), a.k.a. "Superfund Amendments to CERCLA" (1986), which provided a basic definition of "All Appropriate Inquiries" (AAI) prior to property acquisition. SARA made "All Appropriate Inquiries" a condition for "Innocent Landowner" (a.k.a. Innocent Purchaser).

   However, a detailed Rule describing the necessary steps that constituted "All Appropriate Inquiries" was not promulgated at that time. "All Appropriate Inquiries" in SARA focused on:
   a. specialized knowledge or experience of the owner;
   b. relationship of the purchase price to the value of the property;
   c. commonly known or reasonably ascertainable information about the property; and
   d. degree of obviousness of, and the ability to detect, contamination.

3. **Brownfields Amendments:** The "Small Business Liability Relief and Brownfields Revitalization Act" (Public Law 107-118; 115 Stat. 2356), a.k.a. the "Brownfields Amendments" to CERCLA, was enacted January 11, 2002. This was the second revision to CERCLA. Title II—Brownfields Revitalization and Restoration, SubTitle B—Brownfields Liability Clarifications revises CERCLA Section 101(35), clarifying the requirements necessary to establish the Innocent Landowner defense. In addition, the Brownfields Amendments amend CERCLA § 9607 by adding protections (exemptions) against CERLCA liability for Bona Fide Prospective Purchasers and Contiguous Property Owners.

4. **All Appropriate Inquiries:** The Brownfields Amendments mandate that the U.S. EPA promulgate standards and practices *"for the purpose of satisfying the requirement to carry out all appropriate inquiries under § 9601(35)(B)(i)."* The "All Appropriate Inquiries" Final Rule by the U.S. EPA is part of the implementation of the Brownfields Amendments and is codified in Federal Regulation 40 CFR Part 312—Standards and Practices for All Appropriate Inquiries; Final Rule; Tuesday, Nov. 1, 2005.

   This is the first time that detailed environmental "All Appropriate Inquiries" due diligence procedures for purchasers of real estate are codified into federal regulation.

5. **AAI Statutory Objective:** Three different liability protections to commercial/industrial property owners are obtainable (whichever are applicable) by conducting *"all appropriate inquiries into the previous ownership and uses of the property (facility) consistent with good commercial or customary standards and practices"* in order to identify *"conditions indicative of releases or threatened releases of hazardous substances on, at, in or to the property that would be the subject of a response action for which a liability protection would be needed."* These liability protection benefits are also subject to compliance with any and all other CERCLA requirements (Continuing Obligations) that may be relevant to the property.

3

6. **AAI Applicability:**
a. The law is applicable to any nonresidential property for the purpose of obtaining CERCLA liability protection for releases or threatened releases of hazardous substances.

> *"The all appropriate inquiries regulation potentially will apply to most commercial property transactions. The requirements will be applicable to any public or private party, who may potentially claim protection from CERCLA liability. . . ."*

(AAI Final Rule, Section V, A, 1, pg. 66102.)

b. The law is also applicable to those residential properties which serve a commercial function (irrespective of the number of units in a property), as well as to commercial/industrial entities that purchased land for residential development.
c. The law is applicable to all government owned properties (including residential).
d. The law is applicable to U.S. EPA "Brownfields" Grantees under CERCLA Section 104(k)(2)(B). Such grantees, additionally, have broader requirements.

7. **Does Not Address Continuing Obligations:** The "All Appropriate Inquiries" Final Rule regulations only address the "All Appropriate Inquiries" provisions of CERCLA Section 101(35)(B)(i)(I) and 101(35)(B)(ii) and (iii).

The requirements of "Continuing Obligations," including "Reasonable Steps" of CERLCA Section 101(35)(B)(i)(II), are not addressed in the AAI Final Rule. However, interim guidance is found at:

> *Interim Guidance Regarding Criteria Landowners Must Meet in Order to Qualify for Bona Fide Prospective Purchaser, Contiguous Property Owner, or Innocent Landowner Limitations on CERCLA Liability ("Common Elements"), March 6, 2003,*
> *www.epa.gov/compliance/resources/policies/cleanup/superfund/common-elem-guide.pdf*

Additionally, ASTM (Committee E50.02) will be releasing a Standard Practice for Continuing Obligations, expected late 2006. (See also Part IX: Continuing Obligations.)

8. **Hazardous Substances Listings:** CERCLA hazardous substances definitions and substance listings can be found at 42 U.S.C. § 9601(14) and 40 C.F.R. Part 302, Table 302.

[Ref: AAI Final Rule, Section I and Section II, A, B, pg. 66071-72.]

C. CERCLA Landowner Liability Protections

1. **Innocent Landowner (ILO):** The law (Brownfields Amendments) essentially <u>continues (with some clarifications) the existing</u> CERCLA third party "Innocent Landowner Defense" (also known as "Innocent Purchaser Defense") that *"at the time the defendant acquired the facility the defendant did not know and had no reason to know that any hazardous substance that is the subject of a release or threatened release was disposed of on, in, or at the property (facility)."*

    (Note: There are technically other types of Innocent Landowners, i.e., government acquired contaminated property or inheritors of contaminated property. However, the only kind of "innocent landowner" discussed here is the purchaser who unknowingly purchases contaminated property.)

2. **Contiguous Property Owner (CPO):** The law <u>adds</u> CERCLA "Contiguous Property Owner" liability protection for a property owner, by exempting the property owner from CERLCA "owner/operator" status, who did not know of contamination on the property prior to acquisition and contamination is later found to have migrated from an adjoining property. This protects parties that are essentially victims of pollution incidents caused by their neighbor's actions, *"provided that the landowner claiming to be a contiguous property owner can demonstrate that he did not cause, contribute, or consent to any release or threatened release of hazardous substances."*

3. **Bona Fide Prospective Purchaser (BFPP):** The law <u>adds</u> CERCLA "Bona Fide Prospective Purchaser" liability protection for a property owner, by exempting the property owner from CERLCA "owner/operator" status, who knowingly purchases contaminated property *if the prospective purchaser can demonstrate that all on-site contamination occurred prior to acquisition.*

    The statutory language at § 9601(40) defines a Bona Fide Prospective Purchaser (BFPP) as a person (or tenant) that:
    a. acquires ownership after January 11, 2002;
    b. establishes each of the following by a preponderance of the evidence
        i.   all disposal of hazardous substances at the facility occurred before the person acquired the facility;
        ii. the person made *"all appropriate inquiries into the previous ownership and uses of the facility in accordance with generally accepted good commercial and customary standards and practices in accordance with the standards and practices referred to in clauses (ii) and (iv) of paragraph (35)(B). . . ."*

4. **Liability Protection Statutory References:**
    a. If the property is known to be contaminated prior to acquisition, see the "Bona Fide Prospective Purchaser" liability protection. [CERCLA 101(40) and 107(r).]
    b. If the property is not known to be contaminated prior to acquisition, but is later found to be contaminated from prior activities at the property, see the "Innocent Landowner Defense." [CERCLA 101(35) and 107(b)(3).]
    c. If the property is not known to be contaminated prior to acquisition but is later found to be contaminated from activities at adjacent properties, see the "Contiguous Property Owner" liability protection. [CERCLA 107(q).]

[Ref: AAI Final Rule, Section II, D, pg. 66072-74.]
(See Part IX: Continuing Obligations.)

D. Qualifying for the Protections

1. **Pre-Acquisition "Threshold Criteria":** Each of the three landowner liability protections have threshold criteria that must be met prior to property acquisition, in order for a prospective landowner (buyer or Grantee) to qualify for the protection(s) against CERCLA liability. These are usually called "Threshold Criteria."

2. **Post-Acquisition "Continuing Obligations" Requirements:** Each of the three landowner liability protections also have post-acquisition requirements in order to maintain CERCLA liability. These are usually called "Continuing Obligations."

3. **"Common Elements":** Requirements that cut across all the protections are usually called "Common Elements." Common Elements apply to pre- and post-acquisition requirements for all the protections, i.e., "Common Elements" include "Threshold Criteria," as well as "Continuing Obligations."

4. **Basic Threshold Criteria For All Protections:**
   - Perform "All Appropriate Inquiries" (AAI) in accordance with the AAI Final Rule, and prior to property acquisition (title transfer);
   - Demonstrate that not potentially liable for response costs;
   - Demonstrate that not affiliated with any other person who is potentially liable (affiliation is interpreted broadly and includes familial and business contractual, corporate and financial relationships intended to facilitate transactions in order to avoid liability).

   Note: Instead of the last two items above, the Innocent Purchaser requirement is:
   o That the release of hazardous substances and the resulting damages were caused by an act or omission of a third party with whom the person does not have employment, agency or a contractual relationship.
   Other requirements specific only to the innocent landowner defense include:
   o The person exercised due care with respect to the hazardous substance concerned, taking into consideration the characteristics of such hazardous substance, in light of all relevant facts and circumstances.
   o Took precautions against foreseeable acts or omissions of any such third party and the consequences that could foreseeably result from such acts or omissions.
   (AAI Final Rule, Section II, D, 3, pg. 66074.)

5. **Additional Threshold Criteria for Innocent Landowner:**
   - Demonstrate that at the time the defendant (landowner) acquired the facility, the defendant (landowner) did not know and had no reason to know that any hazardous substance that is the subject of a release or threatened release was disposed of on, in or at the facility.

6. **Additional Threshold Criteria for Contiguous Property Owner:**
   - Demonstrate that the landowner did not cause, contribute or consent to any release or threatened release of hazardous substances.

7. **Additional Threshold Criteria for Bona Fide Prospective Purchaser:**
   - Demonstrate that the property was acquired subsequent to all disposal activities involving hazardous substances at the property (which includes not adding any new contamination).

Note: The above discussion includes the "Threshold Criteria." For discussion of "Continuing Obligations," see Part IX: Continuing Obligations.

E. Three Protections for One AAI

Note: The three landowner liability protections are generally abbreviated as follows:
Innocent Landowner—ILO (Also: Innocent Landowner Defense—ILD)
Contiguous Property Owner—CPO
Bona Fide Prospective Purchaser—BFPP

1. **AAI/Phase I Effective for All Three Protections:** All of the CERCLA landowner liability protections (as applicable) are available to prospective landowners of commercial/industrial real estate properties by doing an AAI/Phase I Site Assessment.

2. **One Time Only:** The AAI/Phase I only needs to be conducted once (prior to acquiring title). The same AAI/Phase I is effective for any of the three protections (subject to any and all Continuing Obligations).

3. **Multiple Protections:**
   a. There is no apparent reason why a landowner would not be able to employ more than one protection at the same time, e.g., Innocent Landowner Defense and Contiguous Property Owner Protection.
   b. It is even conceivable that a landowner could use the Innocent Landowner Defense (if the buyer did not know and had no reason to know) for some contamination, while, at the same time, being a Bona Fide Prospective Purchaser regarding other known contamination.

4. **Continuing Obligations Apply to All Protections:** Conducting "All Appropriate Inquiries" alone does not provide a landowner with protection against CERCLA liability. The landowner must also comply with all other statutory post-acquisition requirements (Continuing Obligations) to protect human health and the environment that may apply, as well as Continuing Obligations that were in effect prior to acquisition. (See Part IX: Continuing Obligations.)

F. "Midnight Dumper Insurance"

The first benefit of the "All Appropriate Inquiries" (AAI) landowner liability protection is simply that performing an environmental site assessment prior to property acquisition can provide liability protection if the new property owner *"did not know and had no reason to know"* about any contamination at the time of acquisition. In other words, AAI defines the requirements to become an Innocent Landowner (Innocent Purchaser).

An obvious use of this protection would be a property that had been contaminated by a "midnight dumper" (with or without the knowledge of the then property owner). As long as the new property owner conducted "All Appropriate Inquiries," and *"did not know and had no reason to know,"* the new property owner would have protection (subject to Continuing Obligations).

Since the enactment of SARA in 1986, many property owners have attempted to assert the Innocent Landowner defense, to varying degrees of success. In general, the Innocent Landowner defense should work well where there is no question that the prospective landowner did not know and had no reason to know, e.g., a "midnight dumper" situation. Where a case could be made that the prospective landowner should have known, or at least suspected, about the contamination, the Innocent Landowner defense has not met with a strong record of success.

There is no reason to anticipate any change in this paradigm under the AAI Final Rule. If there is a strong case that there was no reason to know about any contamination, then the Innocent Landowner (or the Contiguous Property owner if the contamination originated from another property) should indeed provide the landowner liability protections available under the law.

As a practical matter, most situations of concern to (prospective) landowners focus on properties where there is some history of industrial activity which may have led to some degree of contamination. In general, for those situations, the Bona Fide Prospective Purchaser is the better vehicle for asserting landowner liability protections.

G. New Incentive "To Know" about Prior Contamination

1. **Bona Fide Prospective Purchaser Protection Requires Knowledge of Contamination:**
    In order to receive the landowner liability protections of the Bona Fide Prospective Purchaser (BFPP), among other requirements, the landowner <u>must demonstrate that all on-site contamination occurred prior to property acquisition.</u>

2. **Incentive "To Know":** <u>The Bona Fide Prospective Purchaser protection significantly encourages prospective landowners to want "to know" about any contamination.</u> This may be particularly compelling where some knowledge or evidence of contamination at the property is already manifested.

3. **Incentive for Sampling and Analysis:** If, in fact, there is a heightened interest to want "to know," it may also be more likely for prospective landowners to consider sampling and analysis, certainly in cases where some knowledge of contamination at the property is apparent within the AAI/Phase I. The AAI Final Rule requires that the scope of the "All Appropriate Inquiries" include the ability to detect the contamination by appropriate investigation.

    Sampling and analysis could be expected to further disclose *"the degree of obviousness of the presence or likely presence of contamination at the property, and the ability to detect the contamination by appropriate investigation."* Sampling and analysis would conceivably be viewed as appropriate documentation as to whether contamination, if any, in fact occurred prior to acquisition.

"For the first time since the enactment of CERCLA in 1980, a person may purchase property with the knowledge that the property is contaminated without being held potentially liable for the cleanup of the contamination."—U.S.EPA (www.epa.gov/swerosps/bf/aai/compare_astm.pdf, page 1, October 2005.)

H. New Incentive to Redevelop Brownfields

1. **Political Motivations:** From a political perspective, the Brownfields/All Appropriate Inquiries landowner liability protections were driven by a desire by Congress to encourage reinvestment, particularly in older industrial properties. Investments in older industrial sites were, until now, hampered with fears that the new owners would be saddled with cleanup costs on account of contamination caused by earlier owners or users of the property.

2. **Business/Environmental Benefits:** The Brownfields AAI paradigm is widely viewed as being both "pro-business" and "pro-environment." Businesses benefit from being relieved of potential liability due to contamination caused by others. In addition, by encouraging business redevelopment of such properties, the landowner liability protections also benefit the environment by reducing the incentive for businesses to develop outlying virgin farmland. As well, redevelopment within established industrial zones lessens urban sprawl.

3. **What Actually Are "Brownfields":** *"With certain legal exclusions and additions, the term 'brownfield site' means real property, the expansion, redevelopment, or reuse of which may be complicated by the presence or potential presence of a hazardous substance, pollutant, or contaminant."* [www.epa.gov/brownfields/glossary.htm]

4. **Low Definition Threshold:** Meeting the above definition is not intended on being difficult:
    a. *". . . may be complicated by"*—i.e., the property doesn't even have to be demonstratively contaminated;
    b. *". . . or potential presence"*—i.e., once again, the property doesn't even have to be demonstratively contaminated;
    c. *". . . be complicated by"*—i.e., there is no severe standard as to how much a property needs to be damaged or "complicated" before it can be considered a Brownfield.

    To be a "Brownfield site," a property also does not have to be vacant, abandoned or idle.

    Note: Based on this definition, many (if not most) commercial/industrial properties may be "Brownfields" regardless of whether individual property owners label their properties as such.

5. **Brownfields Definition Is Useful for Government Funding Programs:** If government funds are desired, then the "Brownfields" status of the property must be documented. The "Brownfields" definition provides a (simple) mechanism to do just that.

Note: Notwithstanding the above, AAI and the landowner liability protections apply to all commercial and industrial properties (regardless of whether the property has the label of "Brownfields" or not).

6. **Government Cleanup of Protected Contaminated Properties:** If the U.S. EPA cleans up (using government funds) contaminated property owned by a Bona Fide Prospective Purchaser, then the U.S. EPA can place a lien on the property for the increase in fair market value attributable to U.S. EPA's response action, or for the unrecovered response costs, whichever is lower. (If the increase in fair market value exceeds the unrecovered response costs, then the current property owner can actually not only not have to pay for any cleanup, but conceivably may reap a profit.) (See AAI Final Rule, Section II, D, 1, pg. 66073.)

I. What's Not Included

Note: Aside from what protections are not included within AAI, the first consideration is simply that AAI, if done improperly, may provide no protection whatsoever. The framework is that AAI will allow a new landowner to become free from Joint and Several Liability. However, Joint and Several Liability is still fully the law of the land. AAI requires proactive efforts to become free from liability. Lacking such proactive effort, the landowner remains burdened with Joint and Several Liability.

1. **AAI Applies to Federal CERLCA Law Only:** This entire discussion of AAI (and the ASTM Phase I) relates only to Federal CERCLA law and has no direct bearing on other federal or state laws. For example, RCRA, wetlands, state hazardous waste laws or state voluntary action programs would not be affected by AAI. It is possible that a landowner may be protected against CERCLA cleanup liability yet remain liable under a state program.

2. **Petroleum Is Not a CERCLA Hazardous Substance:** Petroleum products are not included within CERCLA and are under separate jurisdiction.

3. **Private Actions Not Included:** Private actions, toxic torts, property injury claims, citizen suits, etc., are not part of this paradigm. For example, a landowner could be protected from CERCLA liability but conceivably still be liable to private parties who demonstrate damages under common law.

4. **Business Risk:** Neither AAI nor ASTM deal with, or attempt to protect against, various non-CERCLA related environmental risks. For example, asbestos, lead, radon and mold, etc., can present business risks to a property owner. These can optionally be addressed outside of AAI and the ASTM Phase I. (See also Part L: ASTM Non-CERCLA Considerations.)

5. **Lessee Considerations:** Neither the statute nor the AAI Final Rule addresses any situation other than a person who acquires property ownership and who wants CERLCA protections. There is no provision for lessees. Even for a contract where the lease turns into a sale, there is no provision for AAI to apply unless and until a person acquires ownership. However, a lessee/contaminator can still be liable under CERCLA as an operator of the property.

   As such, if a lessee cannot receive Bona Fide Prospective Purchaser protection yet can be treated as an owner/operator, lessees may need to be careful regarding any (or exacerbation of any) pre-existing contamination and ensure that no further contamination occurs at the property.

6. **Lessor Considerations:** Neither the statute nor the AAI Final Rule addresses the situation where a person acquires a property after performing AAI, and obtains landowner liability protection, and then leases the property to another person who proceeds to contaminate the property.

J. Lender Considerations

Since receiving the Secured Creditor Exemption (1996), many lenders have found that their environmental liability exposure, beyond recouping their capital, does not constitute an inordinate risk. However, common practice among lenders is to generally continue with some degree of environmental due diligence.

Within the lender community, there is currently a range of positions regarding environmental site assessments. Some lenders scrutinize environmental conditions carefully, others less so. Some don't require more than a simple questionnaire except for larger loans. Others refuse outright to lend if a Phase I even just recommends a Phase II.

In addition, since there has been no historical requirement or consensus as to who can be an Environmental Professional, lenders have served as somewhat impartial arbiters of that issue.

With the implementation of the AAI Final Rule, the revised ASTM Phase I and minimum requirements for Environmental Professionals, lender considerations are changing.

1. **Buyer's Liability Protection:** "All Appropriate Inquiries" is the regulation that prospective landowners (buyers) should use in protecting themselves against potential U.S. EPA CERCLA liability. Allowing a buyer to think otherwise is imprudent.
   > *"All Appropriate Inquiries is the process of evaluating a property's environmental conditions and assessing potential liability for any contamination."*
   > — EPA Consumer Fact Sheet on the All Appropriate Inquiries Final Rule.
   > www.epa.gov/Brownfields/aai/aai_final_factsheet.pdf

2. **Buyers and Lenders Have Different Liability Protection Needs:** Buyers (customers) need to understand that "All Appropriate Inquiries" is intended to protect them, while Lender Environmental Risk Management requirements are intended to protect lenders.

3. **Lender Involvement:** The responsibility for the buyer's liability protection lies with the buyer, not with the lender. However, the nature of lender/customer relationships (and traditional involvement in environmental due diligence) gives rise to potential concerns. In particular, a lender would not want a customer to unwisely rely on a lender's environmental risk management for the customer's protection.

4. **Good Commercial Practice:** The ASTM Phase I Standard Practice has been revised for the specific purpose of allowing prospective landowners (buyers) to comply with AAI. The revised ASTM Phase I (ASTM E1527-05) represents good commercial and customary practice.

5. **Prior Phase I Archived:** The prior ASTM Phase I (ASTM E1527-00) has been archived by ASTM. It does not provide AAI landowner liability protections and cannot necessarily be expected to represent good commercial practice (after November 1, 2006). Ordering the "old" Phase I may be problematic.

6. **AAI/Phase I Should Be Conducted by Prospective Landowner:** In order to achieve the AAI landowner liability protections, the prospective landowner should be the responsible party who conducts the AAI/Phase I. (See also Part DD: Prospective Landowner (Buyer) Should Conduct the AAI/Phase I.) A Phase I conducted by a lender without any involvement on the part of the buyer (customer) cannot be expected to provide AAI protection to that buyer.

7. **Other Lender Considerations:** Other items which lenders may want to be aware of include:
   a. **AAI Not Required for Refinancing:** An AAI/Phase I provides no protection for the customer in a refinancing situation. Generally, only the lender's risk management needs are of concern in that situation.
   b. **Reuse of "Old" Phase I Reports:** Phase I reports older than one year (and six months for some items) provide no AAI liability protection to customers unless those reports are updated per specific AAI requirements.
   c. **Using Reports Done By Sellers:** Phase I reports done by sellers may provide no protection to customers unless those reports are reviewed and augmented by the prospective landowner (buyer) per the AAI regulations.

PART II: "ASTM PHASE I" BASICS

Note: To obtain the revised and updated ASTM Phase I Environmental Site Assessment
Standard Practice, call or email ASTM at: 610-832-9585 or service@astm.org

K. ASTM Phase I Background

1. **ASTM:** ASTM International is a standards development organization which uses a consensus based process. "Producers" (e.g., environmental consultants) have equal input into the standards development process as do "users" (e.g., real estate owners and lenders) and "general interest" (e.g., governmental agencies).

2. **ASTM Phase I:** Because SARA (1986) did not provide for a regulation defining in detail the steps required of "All Appropriate Inquiries," ASTM developed a voluntary consensus based Standard Practice. This is known as the "Standard Practice for Environmental Site Assessments: Phase I Environmental Site Assessment Process." (It is commonly referred to as "ASTM Phase I" or even simply as "Phase I.")

3. **ASTM Phase I Standard Practice:** The term "standard" as used by ASTM means a document developed and established within the consensus principle of ASTM.

   The term "practice" means a definitive set of instructions for performing one or more specific operations (excluding specific operations that produce a test result).

   The term "standard practice" is an accepted procedure for the performance of one or more operations and functions.

   The "ASTM Phase I Environmental Site Assessment Process" is a "Standard Practice" for environmental site assessments.

4. **ASTM Phase I Revisions:** The ASTM Phase I was originally developed in 1993 (ASTM E1527-93) and was subsequently revised in 1994 (ASTM E1527-94), revised in 1997 (ASTM E1527-97) and in 2000 (ASTM E1527-00).

5. **ASTM Marketplace Acceptance:** The ASTM Phase I has been widely recognized as providing reasonable procedures regarding how to perform "All Appropriate Inquiries" for CERCLA liability protection. Prior to the AAI Final Rule, it has been widely accepted that the ASTM Phase I Standard Practice actually defined "All Appropriate Inquiries." That has now been vindicated in the AAI Final Rule, being that the prior ASTM Phase I Standard Practices are recognized by U.S. EPA as the interim AAI Standard.

L. ASTM Non-CERCLA Considerations

1. **Petroleum Products:** The ASTM Phase I includes petroleum products within its scope. Petroleum and crude oil are excluded from the definition of CERCLA hazardous substances. However, the marketplace customarily includes petroleum within an environmental site assessment. (ASTM Phase I, E1527-05, Section 1.1.2.)

2. **Business Environmental Risk:** The ASTM Phase I does not include other business environmental risk issues associated with a property. Business environmental risk involves considerations which go beyond the ASTM Phase I Standard Practice, and which are called "Non-Scope Considerations."

    The ASTM Phase I Non-Scope Considerations include:
    *   Asbestos-Containing Building Materials
    *   Radon
    *   Lead-Based Paint
    *   Lead in Drinking Water
    *   Wetlands
    *   Regulatory compliance
    *   Cultural and historic resources
    *   Industrial hygiene
    *   Health and safety
    *   Ecological resources
    *   Endangered species
    *   Indoor air quality
    *   Biological agents
    *   Mold
    (ASTM Phase I, E1527-05, Section 13.1.5.)

Note: "Petroleum Products" is a required element within an ASTM Phase I, even though it is not a CERCLA hazardous substance and is not required for achieving the AAI landowner liability protection.

At the same time, "Non-Scope Considerations" are not required in order to obtain AAI landowner liability protections and are not required within an ASTM Phase I.

M. Limitations of the Prior ASTM Phase I ESA (E1527-00)

With the promulgation of the "All Appropriate Inquiries" Final Rule, the then existing ASTM Phase I (E1527-00), although fundamentally sound (and accepted by U.S. EPA as an interim standard), was found to be lacking in a number of areas as compared to the new AAI requirements.

"We considered ASTM E1527-2000, for use in this rule and determined that the standard is inconsistent with applicable law because it does not meet the statutory criteria necessary to achieve the purpose of the rule." (AAI Proposed Rule, Section II, C, pg. 52545.)

"The ASTM standards do not address all of the required criteria. For example, the ASTM standards do not provide for interviews of past owners, operators and occupants of a facility.

In addition, ASTM's existing standard does not meet other statutory requirements. CERCLA 101(35)(B)(iii)(III) mandates 'Reviews of historical sources, such as chain of title documents, aerial photographs, building department records and land use records, to determine the previous uses and occupancies of the real property since the property was first developed.' ASTM E1527-2000 requires identification of all obvious uses of the property from the present, back to the property's obvious first developed use or back to 1940, whichever is earlier. Congress did not qualify the review to obvious uses, and did not give an alternate date regarding the review.

Further, CERCLA 101(35)(B)(iii)(VI) states that: 'Visual inspections of the facility and adjoining properties' shall be included in the inquiry. ASTM E1527-2000 does not mandate visual inspections of adjoining properties.

CERCLA 101(35)(B)(iii)(VIII) also states that all appropriate inquiries shall include: 'The relationship of the purchase price to the value of the property, if the property was not contaminated.' In its E1527-2000 standard, ASTM limits this requirement to actual knowledge by the defendant. The statute's criteria do not limit this to actual knowledge.

Finally, CERCLA 101(35)(B)(iii)(IV) states that all appropriate inquiries shall include: 'Searches for recorded environmental cleanup liens against the facility that are filed under Federal, State, or local law.' ASTM's E1527-2000 standard describes a much more limited scope for this search than the statute requires.

As a result, use of the ASTM standards would be inconsistent with applicable law."

(AAI Proposed Rule, Section V, I, pg. 52574-75.)

N. ASTM Phase I ESA (E1527-05) Approved by U.S. EPA

1. **ASTM Phase I Conformance With AAI Final Rule:** As directed by the Brownfields Amendments (2002), the U.S. EPA developed and released the All Appropriate Inquiries (AAI) Final Rule. As a consequence of the AAI Final Rule, which identifies per Federal regulation the necessary components of "All Appropriate Inquiries," ASTM has revised the Phase I so as to be in conformance with the Final Rule. The revised ASTM Phase I was released November 18, 2005, as ASTM E1527-05.

2. **ASTM Phase I Referenced in the AAI Final Rule:** The AAI Rule does not require that the revised ASTM Phase I (E1527-05) be used to achieve AAI. However, the U.S. EPA has referenced the "procedures" of the revised ASTM Phase I in the Final Rule as being an acceptable approach to conducting AAI. The AAI Final Rule repeatedly references the ASTM Phase I (E1527-05) procedures as being consistent with the Final Rule.

    > *"The agency (EPA) has determined that this voluntary consensus standard is consistent with (the) final rule and is compliant with the statutory criteria for all appropriate inquiries. Persons conducting all appropriate inquiries may use the procedures included in the ASTM E1527-05 standard to comply with (the) final rule. . . .*

    > *The following industry standards may be used to comply with the requirements set forth in § 312.23 through 312.31 . . . (t)he procedures of ASTM International Standard E1527-05. . . ."*

    (AAI Final Rule, Section IV, F, pg. 66081; Section V, I, pg. 66106; Part 312, Subpart B—Definitions, § 312.11, pg. 66108.)

3. **Performance and Prescriptive Variations:** Neither AAI nor the ASTM Phase I are entirely either performance-based or prescriptive-based. However, in comparison with each other, AAI is more performance-based, and ASTM is more prescriptive-based. The AAI Final Rule indicates "what" needs to be done to satisfy AAI. ASTM identifies reasonable and good commercial practices regarding the conduct of AAI.

    This distinction can be highlighted by the language itself in the AAI and the ASTM Phase I.

    a. The U.S. EPA recognizes the AAI Final Rule as being a "performance standard."
        > *"We are retaining the proposed performance factors and objectives in the final rule. We continue to believe, as did many commenters, that basing the regulations on a set of overall performance factors and specific objectives lends clarity and flexibility to the standards. Such an approach also allows for the application of professional judgment and expertise to account for site-specific circumstances."*
        (AAI Final Rule, Section IV, L, pg. 66086.)

        > *"Commenters were concerned that the proposed performance-based approach would make it more difficult to qualify for the CERLCA liability protections than an approach that requires strict adherence to prescriptive data gathering requirements that do not allow for the application of professional judgment. However, the vast majority of commenters who commented on the performance-based nature of the proposed rule supported the proposed approach."* (AAI Final Rule, Section III, Summary of Comments and Changes from Proposed Rule to Final Rule, pg. 66075.)

    b. On the other hand, the revised ASTM Phase I is based on *"a set of instructions for performing one or more specific operations and should be supplemented by education, experience and professional judgment."*
        (ASTM Phase I, E1527-05, Section 1.6, underlining added. See also Section 4.3.)

    c. In effect, the revised ASTM Phase I Standard Practice (E1527-05) provides a set of instructions, or a "standard practice," which assists Environmental Professionals and the regulated community in meeting the broad performance-based requirements of AAI with a heightened degree of confidence.

4. **Why an AAI Should Be Done Using the ASTM Standard Practice:** For a prospective landowner desirous of protecting his or her investment against CERLCA liability, the optimal scenario, even though use of the ASTM Phase I is technically optional, is to conduct the AAI/Phase I so that it meets the AAI Final Rule plus having it done per the ASTM Phase I Standard Practice.

    a. U.S. EPA/AAI approves the ASTM Phase I procedures. Using the ASTM Phase I procedures provides heightened security that conclusions and recommendations will not be challenged by the U.S. EPA.

    b. The ASTM Standard provides a large degree of flexibility to the Environmental Professional.

    Note: In addition, selecting a P.E. or P.G. as the Environmental Professional may add immeasurably to the defensibility of the AAI, being that the U.S. EPA, in the AAI Final Rule Preamble, indicates confidence in favor of the use of state-licensed Environmental Professionals.

5. **Can an AAI Be Only Partially Done Per the ASTM Phase I Standard Practice?** If an AAI is done per the ASTM Phase I Standard Practice (E1527-05) must the entire AAI conform to the standard practice? There is nothing in either the Final Rule or in the ASTM Phase I that specifically addresses this question. However, there is nothing to suggest that this is prohibited either.

    In addition, the AAI Final Rule repeatedly reaffirms that the Environmental Professional has flexibility, in terms of professional judgment, regarding the specifics of conducting an AAI.

    The language in the AAI Final Rule states that *"persons conducting all appropriate inquiries may use the procedures included in the ASTM E1527-05 standard to comply. . . ."* Being that these ASTM procedures are voluntary and optional, there appears to be no reason why Environmental Professionals cannot use their professional judgment regarding which procedures of the ASTM Phase I should be used for a particular circumstance.

O. ASTM & AAI Terminology Distinctions

"Phase I" and "All Appropriate Inquiries" are commonly interchanged terms. In practice, since the ASTM Phase I has historically been used to assert the "Innocent Purchaser" landowner defense, and the revised ASTM Phase I is intended to establish the AAI Final Rule landowner liability protections, the terms "Phase I" and "All Appropriate Inquiries" (AAI) continue to frequently be interchanged in common usage as if they are entirely identical. However, each of the following terms is uniquely defined (even if the marketplace interchanges them):

1. **"All Appropriate Inquiries (AAI)":** <u>Statutory/regulatory term</u> for achieving U.S. EPA CERCLA liability protections. The purpose of an AAI is to *"identify releases and threatened releases of hazardous substances on, at, in, or to the property that would be the subject of a response action for which a liability protection would be needed. . . ."*

2. **"Phase I Environmental Site Assessment":** <u>ASTM term</u> for determining whether a site has recognized environmental conditions (RECs). Identifying RECs constitutes the ASTM standard practice for Environmental Site Assessments.

   "Objective—The purpose of this Phase I Environmental Site Assessment is to identify, to the extent feasible pursuant to the processes prescribed herein, 'recognized environmental conditions' in connection with the property (see 1.1.1)." (ASTM Phase I, E1527-05, Section 7.1.)

3. **"Environmental Due Diligence":** A more general term to describe the process of inquiry into the environmental characteristics of a property. ASTM defines "Due Diligence" as:

   "the process of inquiring into the environmental characteristics of a parcel of commercial real estate or other conditions, usually in connection with a commercial real estate transaction. <u>The degree and kind of due diligence vary for different properties and differing purposes.</u>" (ASTM Phase I, E1527-05, Section 3.2.25, underlining added.)

4. **"User":** ASTM term for the person seeking an environmental site assessment of the property. It includes AAI prospective landowners or grantees. It also includes others who may desire to conduct an assessment but who have no direct relationship to the AAI protections, e.g., potential tenants, property managers or lenders.

5. **"Recognized Environmental Conditions":** ASTM retains its own term "Recognized Environmental Conditions" and its associated definition.

   "In defining a standard of good commercial and customary practice for conducting an environmental site assessment of a parcel of property, the goal of the processes established by this practice is to identify recognized environmental conditions. The term 'recognized environmental conditions' means the presence or likely presence of any hazardous substances or petroleum products on a property under conditions that indicate an existing release, a past release, or a material threat of a release of any hazardous substances or petroleum products into structures on the property or into the ground, groundwater, or surface water of the property. The term includes hazardous substances or petroleum products even under conditions in compliance with laws." (ASTM Phase I, E1527-05, Section 1.1.1.)

ASTM defines the process of identifying "Recognized Environmental Conditions" as what constitutes the standard of good commercial/industrial and customary practice for Environmental Site Assessments (ASTM Phase I, E1527-05, Sections 1.2, 3.2.76, 4.1, 7.1).

Note 1: The AAI Final Rule doesn't use the term "Recognized Environmental Conditions." Once again, it uses the phrase *"identification of conditions indicative of releases or threatened releases of hazardous substances on, at, in, or to the subject property."* However, the two phrases are generally understood to represent similar conditions, except only for petroleum.

Note 2: ASTM also utilizes a related term called "Historical Recognized Environmental Conditions." A historical REC is used to describe a situation which in the past would have been a REC, but which, regarding the current Phase I, may no longer be a REC. For example, site contamination which has been remediated would no longer be a REC but would instead be reclassified as a historical REC.

6. **"Material Threat":** The revised ASTM Phase I indicates that a "material threat" of a release is a "recognized environmental condition." "Material Threat" is defined as a *"physically observable or obvious threat which is reasonably likely to lead to a release that, in the opinion of the environmental professional, is threatening and might result in impact to public health or the environment."* (ASTM Phase I, E1527-05, Section 3.2.53.)

7. **U.S. EPA Language:** The U.S. EPA uses the following language to explain the difference between "All Appropriate Inquiries" and other environmental assessments:

    "An essential step in real property transactions may be evaluating a property for potential environmental contamination and assessing potential liability for contamination present at the property. The process for assessing properties for the presence or potential presence of environmental contamination often is referred to as 'environmental due diligence,' or 'environmental site assessment.' The Comprehensive Environmental Response Compensation and Liability Act (CERCLA), or Superfund, provides for a similar, but legally distinct, process referred to as 'all appropriate inquiries.'" (AAI Final Rule, Section II, B, pg. 66072.)

P. ASTM Phase I Paragraphs with Major Changes

Although there are numerous changes throughout the revised ASTM Phase I, the following represents a list of paragraphs with major changes. This list is organized by paragraph numbering in the <u>revised</u> ASTM Phase I Standard Practice.

Q. ASTM Phase I ESA May Not Always Be "All Appropriate Inquiries"

1. **ASTM Phase I Conforms to AAI:** ASTM has revised its Phase I Standard Practice to comply with the AAI Final Rule. The U.S. EPA has referenced the revised ASTM Phase I (E1527-05), which allows the ASTM procedures to be used to comply with AAI (although there is no requirement to use the ASTM Phase I).

2. **ASTM Phase I Also Usable for Non-AAI Purposes:** However, the ASTM Phase I is a voluntary industry Standard Practice which is used for a broader range of objectives than just "All Appropriate Inquiries."

ASTM describes its Phase I Environmental Site Assessment as follows:

"*1.1 Purpose—The purpose of this practice is to define good commercial and customary practice in the United States of America for conducting an 'environmental site assessment' of a parcel of commercial real estate with respect to the range of contaminants within the scope of Comprehensive Environmental Response, Compensation and Liability Act (CERCLA) (42 U.S.C. § 9601) and petroleum products.*

3.2.30 environmental site assessment (ESA)—The process by which a person or entity seeks to determine if a particular parcel of real property (including improvements) is subject to recognized environmental conditions. At the option of the user, an 'environmental site assessment' may include more inquiry than that constituting all appropriate inquiry or, if the user is not concerned about qualifying for the LLPs [landowner liability protections], less inquiry than that constituting all appropriate inquiry.

3.2.62 Phase I Environmental Site Assessment—The process described in this practice.

1.1 Purpose— . . . As such, this practice is intended to permit a user to satisfy one of the requirements to qualify for the innocent landowner, contiguous property owner or bona fide prospective purchaser limitations on CERCLA liability (hereinafter, the 'landowner liability protections,' or 'LLPs'): that is, the practice that constitutes 'all appropriate inquiry into the previous ownership and uses of the property consistent with good commercial or customary practice' as defined at 42 U.S.C. § 9601 (35)(B).

4.1 Uses— . . . While use of this practice is intended to constitute all appropriate inquiry for the purposes of the LLPs [landowner liability protections], it is not intended that its use be limited to that purpose.

4.2.1 Use Not Limited to CERCLA—This practice is designed to assist the user in developing information about the environmental condition of a property and as such has utility for a wide range of persons, including those who may have no actual or potential CERCLA liability and/or may not be seeking the LLPs [landowner liability protections].

6.7 Other—Either the user shall make known to the environmental professional the reason why the user wants to have the Phase I Environmental Site Assessment performed or, if the user does not identify the purpose of the Phase I Environmental Site Assessment, the environmental professional shall assume the purpose is to qualify for an LLP [landowner liability protection] to CERLCA liability and state this in the report."

(ASTM Phase I, E1527-05, underlining and quotation marks added.)

R. ASTM & AAI & EP Interrelationships

1. **Did the <u>Prior</u> ASTM Phase I Standard Practices <u>Define</u> "All Appropriate Inquiries" (prior to Nov 1, 2006)?**

"Yes." The U.S. EPA has indicated in the AAI Final Rule that the 1997 and 2000 versions of the ASTM Phase I constituted the interim standard until November 1, 2006.

2. **Does the <u>Revised</u> ASTM Phase I (ASTM E1527-05) <u>Define</u> "All Appropriate Inquiries" (after Nov. 1, 2006)?**

The answer appears to be "Mostly (but not entirely) No." "All Appropriate Inquiries" is defined by the U.S. EPA AAI Final Rule, and not by an ASTM voluntary consensus standard practice. Per the AAI Final Rule (and per ASTM), using the ASTM Phase I (E1527-05) after November 1, 2006 is optional and voluntary.

On the other hand, the ASTM Phase I Standard Practice does influence "All Appropriate Inquiries," even if it does not provide the ultimate definition of "All Appropriate Inquiries." At a minimum, AAI requires that inquiries be done per "good commercial and customary practice." ASTM fills that void.

ASTM, for its part, states that its objectives are to "clarify" and "define" "All Appropriate Inquiries":

> *"Objectives guiding the development of this practice are . . . (3) to ensure that the standard of all appropriate inquiry is practical and reasonable, and (4) to clarify an industry standard for all appropriate inquiry in an effort to guide legal interpretation of the LLPs [landowner liability protections]."* (ASTM Phase I, E1527-05, Section 1.2.)

> *"Practice E1527 has been developed to define 'all appropriate inquiry' for purposes of establishing any of the three LLPs [landowner liability protections] available under CERCLA as amended by the Brownfields Amendments."* (ASTM Phase I, E1527-05, Appendix X1.)

3. **Does AAI Change the Traditional Role of the Environmental Consultant?**

Since CERLCA was enacted, all decision-making powers were essentially in the hands of the U.S. EPA, and environmental consultants usually were somewhat limited to providing services per EPA instructions. With the Brownfields Amendments, and the promulgation of the AAI Final Rule, Environmental Professionals have been designated as the lead party responsible for conducting "All Appropriate Inquiries." In particular, Environmental Professionals have been granted, by regulation, a heightened role and degree of responsibility regarding the conduct of "All Appropriate Inquiries." For example:

   a. EPs are required to give opinions, and, presumably, if those opinions are reasonable and in accordance with the performance factors, those opinions should not be easily overturned;
   b. An EP who performed AAI in accordance with the Performance Factors, but still "missed something," hasn't necessarily invalidated the AAI liability protections;
   c. An EP who could not close Data Gaps hasn't necessarily invalidated the AAI; and
   d. EPs are given latitude as to numerous decisions, e.g., what historical documents to search, minimum search distances for government records, occupants to interview, type and content of questions, how to inspect a property, determining the best process, report format, need for additional investigation, recommendations regarding Phase II sampling and analysis, etc.

4. **What About the Role of the EP Regarding Continuing Obligations?** The common understanding is that the "All Appropriate Inquiries" is done prior to property acquisition (and done by an EP), while Continuing Obligations come into effect subsequent to property acquisition.

However, it is not clear, as defined by regulation, what the role of an EP actually is, regarding Continuing Obligations subsequent to property acquisition. For example:

   a. If anything, it is unclear when Continuing Obligations even commence in the first instance. A property owner may not even be able to comply with any Continuing Obligations without first performing Phase II sampling and analysis (and perhaps resampling and continuing analysis). As such, a Phase II may be an integral part of Continuing Obligations.

   b. The AAI Final Rule does not discourage Phase II sampling and analysis within the "All Appropriate Inquiries" done prior to property acquisition. Quite the contrary. If Phase II sampling and analysis begins within the "All Appropriate Inquiries," then it may be the case that Continuing Obligations (and the direct involvement of the Environmental Professional) also begin within the "All Appropriate Inquiries."

   c. ASTM, for its part, specifically allows for Additional Services, including "remediation techniques" and "more detailed conclusions," if so specified in the terms of engagement between the user and the Environmental Professional. (ASTM Phase I, E1527-05, Section 12.9.)

   d. As such, the perception that Continuing Obligations begin only subsequent to property acquisition, and are totally distinct from "All Appropriate Inquiries" may be simplistic. Continuing Obligations may well begin within the "All Appropriate Inquiries," and may be defined by the professional judgment of the Environmental Professional as much as by the U.S. EPA.

Note: ASTM committee E50.02 is expected to release a standard practice dealing with Continuing Obligations in late 2006.

(See also Part IX: Continuing Obligations.)

5. **Conclusions**

   a. To one degree or another, the functions of the U.S. EPA regarding "All Appropriate Inquiries" have been somewhat "privatized."

   b. The ASTM Phase I has, on the one hand, lost its standing as "the standard" because it simply doesn't have the legal status of an EPA Rule. On the other hand, by being referenced in the AAI Final Rule, the ASTM Phase I has considerable new influence to guide the practice and legal interpretations of "All Appropriate Inquiries."

   c. Environmental Professionals have a new found increased role regarding "All Appropriate Inquiries," and perhaps also regarding Continuing Obligations.

PART III: ENVIRONMENTAL PROFESSIONALS

S. Minimum Educational & Experience Requirements

1. **Definition:** An Environmental Professional is defined by AAI as:

   "a person who possesses sufficient specific education, training and experience necessary to exercise professional judgment to develop opinions and conclusions regarding conditions indicative of releases of threatened releases on, at, in, or to a property, sufficient to meet the objectives and performance factors in § 312.20(e) and (f)."

2. **Minimum Requirements:** The AAI Final Rule provides for several options which are available in order to qualify as an Environmental Professional (40 CFR Part 312.10). The minimum educational and experience requirements are as follows:

   - *"Hold a current Professional Engineer's (P.E.) or Professional Geologist's (P.G.) license or registration from a state, tribe, or U.S. territory and have the equivalent of three (3) years of full-time relevant experience; or*
   - *Be licensed or certified by the federal government, a state, tribe or U.S. territory to perform environmental inquiries as defined in § 312.21 and have the equivalent of three (3) years of full-time relevant experience; or*
   - *Have a Baccalaureate or higher degree from an accredited institution of higher education in a discipline of engineering or science and the equivalent five (5) years of full-time relevant experience; or*
   - *Have the equivalent of ten (10) years of full-time relevant experience."*

3. **Relevant Experience:** The definition of "relevant experience" is:

   "participation in the performance of all appropriate inquiries investigations, environmental site assessments or other site investigations that may include environmental analyses, investigations and remediation which involve the understanding of surface and subsurface environmental conditions and the processes used to evaluate these conditions and for which professional judgment was used to develop opinions regarding conditions indicative of releases or threatened releases (see § 312.1(c)) to the subject property."

4. **No Professional or Other Private Certifications:** The AAI Final Rule does not recognize Environmental Professionals who are certified or licensed through any professional or other private certification programs and does not recognize or reference any professional certification standards. There are a number of well-established and widely recognized professional certification programs in the U.S. professional arena. However, none of them are recognized by the AAI Final Rule. (Note: The U.S. EPA did not want to get into the business of assessing and monitoring the many available professional certifications.)

   The AAI Final Rule only recognizes (a) government licenses, (b) educational degrees, (c) relevant experience.

5. **Continuing Education:** The requirement for continuing education is:

   "an environmental professional should remain current in his or her field through participation in continuing education or other activities . . . (and) be able to demonstrate such efforts."

[Ref: AAI Final Rule, Subpart B—Definitions, § 312.10, pg. 66108 and Section IV, E, pg. 66079-80.]

T. Qualifications: Additional Considerations

1. **Declarations:** The Environmental Professional must declare, at the end of each report, that:
    "I (We) have the specific qualifications based on education, training and experience to assess a property of the nature, history and setting of the subject property."

2. **Licensed Professionals:** The AAI Final Rule suggests a preference for licensed environmental professionals, and in particular, licensed Professional Engineers (P.E.s) and licensed Professional Geologists (P.G.s):
    "The rigor of the tribal and state-licensed P.E. and P.G. certification processes, including the educational and training requirements, as well as the examination requirements, paired with the requirement to have three years of relevant professional experience conducting all appropriate inquiries <u>will ensure</u> that all appropriate inquiries are conducted under the supervision or responsible charge of an individual <u>well qualified</u> to oversee the collection and interpretation of site-specific information and render informed opinions and conclusions regarding the environmental conditions at a property. . . . The Agency's decision to recognize tribal and state-licensed P.E.s and P.G.s reflects the fact that tribal governments and state legislatures hold such professionals responsible (legally and ethically) for safeguarding public safety, public health and the environment." (AAI Final Rule, Section IV, E, pg. 66079, underlining added.)

    With regard to Environmental Professionals who are not licensed by their state (or tribe):
    ". . . individuals with these qualifications <u>most likely</u> will possess sufficient specific education, training and experience necessary to exercise professional judgment to develop opinions and conclusions regarding conditions indicative of releases or threatened releases on, at, in, or to a property. . . ." (AAI Final Rule, Section IV, E, pg. 66080, underlining added.)

3. **No Preemption of State Professional Licensing Requirements:** *"The definition of environmental professional provided above does not preempt state professional licensing or registration requirements such as those for a professional geologist, engineer, or site remediation professional. Before commencing work, a person should determine the applicability of state professional licensing or registration laws to the activities to be undertaken as part of the inquiry. . . ."* (AAI Final Rule, Subpart B—Definitions and References, § 312.10 "Definitions and References" (b), pg. 66108.)

4. **ASTM—Employees:** ASTM permits an employee of the user, who otherwise qualifies, to be the Environmental Professional (ASTM Phase I, E1527-05, Section 3.2.29).

5. **Professional Certifications:** Although the minimum qualifications to be an Environmental Professional are based only on education and experience, the credentials and certifications provided by established certification bodies nonetheless helps demonstrate that an individual has *"the specific qualifications based on education, training and experience. . ."* which is the required declaration to be made by the Environmental Professional at the conclusion of each AAI report. As just one of many good examples, the Board Certified Environmental Engineer designation of the American Academy of Environmental Engineers would be such a certification.

    In addition, a new association intended to focus specifically on Brownfield professionals is the "Institute of Brownfields Professionals (IBP)". The IBP provides a designation called "Registered Brownfield Professional" to individuals who meet the Institute's established criteria.

U. **Associate Workers**

1. **Under Supervision of EPs:** In general, individuals not meeting the definition of an Environmental Professional may contribute to some aspects of the research or the inquiry, as long as they are working under the supervision or responsible charge of an individual who meets the definition of an Environmental Professional.

   "A person who does not qualify as an environmental professional under the foregoing definition may assist in the conduct of all appropriate inquiries in accordance with this part if such person is under the supervision or responsible charge of a person meeting the definition of an environmental professional provided above when conducting such activities." (AAI Final Rule, Subpart B—Definitions and References, § 312.10 "Definitions and References" (b), pg. 66108.)

   Note: This provision is also relevant to government offices, where, in the past, persons in one office have "signed off" on assessments done by others without supervision or direct involvement.

2. **Property Inspections:** Specifically regarding property inspections, the U.S. EPA recommends (but does not mandate) that the visual inspections of the subject property and adjoining properties be conducted by an Environmental Professional (and not just an individual under the supervision or responsible charge of an Environmental Professional).

   [See also Part OO: Inspection Requirements for the Subject Property.]

   Note: The following may represent a prudent protocol:
   a. Should **be done only by** an Environmental Professional
      - Visually inspect the subject property and adjoining properties.
        Note: Neither the AAI Final Rule nor ASTM require this.
        However, the U.S. EPA Preamble to the Final Rule does recommend this.

   b. Should (at least) **be done under the supervision and responsible charge of** the EP.
      - Interview past and present owners, operators and occupants of the facility for the purpose of gathering information regarding the potential for contamination at the facility.
      - Review historical sources of information such as (but not limited to) chain of title documents, aerial photographs, building department records and land use records, to determine previous uses and occupancies of the real property since the property was first developed.
      - Review Federal, Tribal, State and Local government records, waste disposal records, underground storage tank records and hazardous waste handling, generation, treatment, disposal and spill records, concerning contamination at or near the facility.
      - Include the degree of obviousness of the presence or likely presence of contamination at the property, and the ability to detect the contamination by appropriate investigation.

   c. Should (at least) **be reviewed by** the Environmental Professional
      - Search for recorded environmental cleanup liens against the facility that are filed under Federal, Tribal, State or Local law. (May be done by purchaser or title company.)
      - Include any specialized knowledge or experience on the part of the defendant (buyer).
      - Include relationship of purchase price to value of the property as if not contaminated.
      - Include commonly known or reasonably ascertainable information about the property.

V. Professional Judgment

1. The activities of the Environmental Professional are to be done per his/her *"professional judgment, in accordance with generally accepted good commercial and customary standards and practices."*

2. Both the AAI Final Rule and the revised ASTM Phase I repeatedly indicate that much decision-making within "All Appropriate Inquiries" depends on the professional judgment of the Environmental Professional.

    Example areas where AAI Professional Judgment is highlighted includes:
    Performance Factors
    Work by EPs versus Employees/Subs
    Practically Reviewable Information
    Historical Research—How Far Back?
    Minimum Search Distances
    Data Gaps
    Inspection Physical Limitations
    Occupants to Be Interviewed
    Prior Occupants
    Type and Content of Interview Questions
    Degree of Obviousness
    Determining the Best Investigative Process
    Report Format
    Professional Opinion
    Conformance Declarations

    As well, many specific items within the ASTM Phase I Standard Practice are equally dependant on Professional Judgment. For example:
    ASTM Phase I (3.2.53) Material Threat
    ASTM Phase I (1.6 & 4.3) Professional Judgment
    ASTM Phase I (8.1.3 & 8.3.2) Records Reviews
    ASTM Phase I (8.2.2) Local Records
    ASTM Phase I (7.5.1) Site Reconnaissance & Interviews
    ASTM Phase I (10.5.4) Duplicative Information
    ASTM Phase I (12.6.1 & 12.9) Phase II Trigger
    ASTM Phase I (4.3) Who May Conduct

W. Performance Factors

1. **Performance Factors Regulatory Requirements:** *"(1) Gather the information that is required for each standard and practice . . . that is publicly available, obtainable from its source within reasonable time and cost constraints, and which can practically be reviewed; and*
(2) review and evaluate the thoroughness and reliability of the information gathered in complying with each standard and practice . . . taking into account information gathered in the course of complying with the other standards and practices of this subpart. (In complying with § 312.20(f)(2), if the environmental professional or person conducting the inquiries determines through such review and evaluation that the information is either not thorough or not reliable, then further inquiries should be made to ensure that the information gathered is both thorough and reliable. The performance factors are provided as guidelines to be followed in conjunction with the final objectives for the all appropriate inquiries.)"
(AAI Final Rule, Subpart C—Standards and Practices, § 312.20 "All Appropriate Inquiries" (f), pg. 66109; and Section IV, L, pg. 66087.)

2. **Considerations for Developing Opinions:** *"The opinion provided by an environmental professional regarding the environmental condition of a property and included in the all appropriate inquiries report should be based upon a balance of all information collected."* (AAI Final Rule, Section IV, W, pg. 66100.)
Note: See also Part VV: Commonly Known or Reasonably Ascertainable Information and WW: Degree of Obviousness.

3. **ASTM—Uncertainty Not Eliminated:** *"No environmental site assessment can wholly eliminate uncertainty regarding the potential for recognized environmental conditions in connection with a property. Performance of this practice is intended to reduce, but not eliminate, uncertainty regarding the potential for recognized environmental conditions in connection with a property, and this practice recognizes reasonable limits of time and costs."* (ASTM Phase I, E1527-05, Section 4.5.1.)

4. **ASTM—Environmental Professional Judgment:** *"No practical standard can be designed to eliminate the role of judgment and the value and need for experience in the party performing the inquiry. The professional judgment of an environmental professional is, consequently, vital to the performance of all appropriate inquiry."* (ASTM Phase I, E1527-05, Section 4.3.)

". . . the report shall include the environmental professional's judgment about the significance of the listing [records review listings or other sources of information] *to the analysis of recognized environmental conditions in connection with the property. . . ."* (ASTM Phase I, E1527-05, Section 8.1.9.)

5. **ASTM—No Verification:** *"An environmental professional is not required to verify independently the information provided but may rely on information provided unless he or she has actual knowledge that certain information is incorrect or unless it is obvious that certain information is incorrect. . . ."* (ASTM Phase I, E1527-05, Section 7.5.2.1.)

6. **ASTM—Accuracy and Completeness of Records Review Information:** *"Accuracy and completeness of record information varies among information sources, including governmental sources. Record information is often inaccurate or incomplete. The user or environmental professional is not obligated to identify mistakes or insufficiencies in information provided . . . ."* (ASTM Phase I, E1527-05, Section 8.1.3.)

X. How Much Research Is Enough?

1. **Effort and Process:** *"Exhaustive and costly efforts do not have to be made to access all available sources of data and find every piece of data and information about a property, nor does the rule require that duplicative information be sought from multiple sources. . . . Although compliance with the all appropriate inquiries requirement ultimately will be determined in court, the final rule allows the prospective landowner or grantee and environmental professional to determine the best process and sequence for collecting and analyzing all required information. The sequence of activities and the sources of information used to collect any required information is left to the judgment and expertise of the environmental professional, provided that the overall objectives and the performance factors established for the final rule are met."* (AAI Final Rule, Section IV, L, pg. 66086-87.)

2. **Additional Language from the Original Proposed AAI Rule:** *"EPA and the negotiated rulemaking committee are not suggesting that the goal of the conduct of the all appropriate inquiries is to identify every available document and piece of information regarding a property and the environmental conditions on the property. Instead, the objective of the conduct of 'all appropriate inquiries' is to develop an understanding of the conditions of the property and determine whether or not there are conditions indicative of releases and threatened releases of hazardous substances (and pollutants, contaminants, controlled substances and petroleum and petroleum products, if applicable) on, at, in, or to the subject property."* (Proposed AAI Rule, Section II, E, pg. 52559, 8/26/04.)

3. **Collecting Information:** *". . . the final rule allows that an all appropriate inquiries investigation need not address each of the regulatory criterion in any particular sequence. In addition, information relevant to more than one criterion need not be collected twice. And a single source of information may satisfy the requirement of more than one criterion and more than one objective."* (AAI Final Rule, Section IV, L, pg. 66086.)

4. **User Circumstances:** The AAI Final Rule emphasizes that "All Appropriate Inquiries" is shaped by the unique circumstances of the prospective landowner:
    "Certain aspects of the all appropriate inquiries investigation are specific to the current prospective landowner . . . ." (AAI Final Rule, Section IV, J, pg. 66084.)

    "Some of the statutory criteria are inherently the responsibility of the prospective landowner."
    (AAI Final Rule, Section IV, H, pg. 66082, underlining added.)

    "All appropriate inquiries, as outlined in § 312.20, are not complete unless the results of the inquiries take into account the relevant and applicable specialized knowledge and experience of the persons responsible for undertaking the inquiry [prospective landowners or grantees]." (AAI Final Rule, Subpart C—Standards and Practices, § 312.28 "Specialized Knowledge or Experience on the Part of the Defendant" (b), pg. 66112.)

5. **ASTM—Level of Inquiry Is Variable:** *"Not every property will warrant the same level of assessment. Consistent with good commercial or customary practice, the appropriate level of environmental site assessment will be guided by the type of property subject to assessment, the expertise and risk tolerance of the user and the information developed in the course of the inquiry."* (ASTM Phase I, E1527-05, Section 4.5.3.)

6. **ASTM—Not Exhaustive (General):** *"'All appropriate inquiry' does not mean an exhaustive assessment of a clean property. . . . One of the purposes of this practice is to identify a balance between the competing goals of limiting the costs and time demands inherent in performing an environmental site assessment and the reduction of uncertainty about unknown conditions resulting from additional information."* (ASTM Phase I, E1527-05, Section 4.5.2.)

7. **ASTM—Not Exhaustive (Historical Research):**
    "Uses of the property— . . . This task requires reviewing only as many of the standard historical sources . . . as are necessary and both reasonably ascertainable and likely to be useful. . . ." (ASTM Phase I, E1527-05, Section 8.3.2.)

    "Data Failure— . . . Data failure occurs when all of the standard historical sources that are reasonably ascertainable and likely to be useful have been reviewed and yet the objectives have not been met. Data failure is not uncommon. . . ." (ASTM Phase I, E1527-05, Section 8.3.2.3.)

    "Uses of the property—it would not be required to review them [standard sources of information regarding uses of the property] *unless they were both reasonably ascertainable and likely to be useful. . . ."*
    (ASTM Phase I, E1527-05, Section 8.3.2.)

    "Other historical sources specified in 8.3.4.9 may be used to satisfy the objectives, but are not required to comply with this practice." (ASTM Phase I, E1527-05, Section 8.3.2.3.)

    ". . . (C)hecking 'other historical sources' (see 8.3.4.9) is not required." (ASTM Phase I, E1527-05, Section 8.3.2.)

8. **ASTM—Not Exhaustive (Records Review):** *". . . The user or environmental professional is not obligated to identify, obtain, or review every possible record that might exist with respect to a property . . . Record information that is reasonably ascertainable means (1) information that is publicly available, (2) information that is obtainable from its source within reasonable time and costs constraints, and (3) information that is practically reviewable."* (ASTM Phase I, E1527-05, Section 8.1.4. See also Sections 8.1.4.1, 8.1.4.2 and 8.1.4.3.)

9. **ASTM—Reasonably Ascertainable & Practically Reviewable Records Information:**
    "Reasonably ascertainable—[is] information that is (1) publicly available, (2) obtainable from its source within reasonable time and cost constraints, and (3) practically reviewable."

    "Reasonable time and costs—reasonable time and costs constraints means that the information will be provided by the source within 20 calendar days . . . at no more than a nominal cost. . . ."

    "Practically reviewable— . . . [is] information relevant to the property without the need for extraordinary analysis of irrelevant data. The form of the information shall be such that the user can review the records for a limited geographic area . . . when so much data is generated that it cannot be feasibly reviewed for its impact on the property, it is not practically reviewable."

    (ASTM Phase I, E1527-05, Sections 3.2.73, 3.2.65, 8.1.4, 8.1.4.1, 8.1.4.2 and 8.1.4.3.)

Y. Data Gaps

1. **Data Gap Definition:** *"A lack of or inability to obtain information required by the standards and practices listed in the regulation, despite good faith efforts by the environmental professional or the prospective landowner (or grant recipient) to gather such information pursuant to the objectives for all appropriate inquiries."* (AAI Final Rule, Section IV, N, pg. 66088 and Subpart B—Definitions, § 312.10, pg. 66108.)

2. **Data Gaps Due to Historical Sources:** *"If a search of historical sources of information results in an inability of the environmental professional to document previous uses and occupancies of the property as far back in history as it can be shown that the property contained structures or was placed into use of some form, and such information is not acquired elsewhere during the investigation, then it must be documented as a data gap to the inquiries."* (AAI Final Rule, Section IV, Q, pg. 66091.)

    Note: When data gaps result from a failure to achieve historical research objectives, ASTM refers to this type of data gap as "data failure."

3. **Data Gaps Due to Buyer Not Furnishing Information to EP:**
    "The statute does not mandate that a prospective landowner provide all information to an environmental professional. . . . Any information not furnished to the environmental professional by the prospective landowner that may affect the environmental professional's ability to render such an opinion may be identified by the environmental professional as a 'data gap.'" (AAI Final Rule, Section IV, H, pg. 66082.)

    "(T)he final rule does not require the prospective landowner (or grantee) to provide the information collected as part of the 'additional inquiries' to the environmental professional. . . . Should the required information not be provided to the environmental professional, the environmental professional should assess the impact that the lack of such information may have on his or her ability to render an opinion with regard to conditions indicative of releases or threatened releases of hazardous substances on, at, in or to the property. If the lack of information does impact the ability of the environmental professional to render an opinion with regard to the environmental conditions of the property, the environmental professional should note the missing information as a data gap in the written report."

    (AAI Final Rule, Section III, pg. 66076.)

4. **ASTM—User (Buyer) Not Furnishing Information to EP:** *"User's Obligations—The environmental professional shall note in the report whether or not the user has reported to the environmental professional information pursuant to Section 6 (User's Responsibilities)."* (ASTM Phase I, E1527-05, Section 7.3.2.)

5. **Other Data Gaps:** Data gaps can also result from incompleteness in any other activities, e.g., inability to inspect the property or adjoining properties, conduct interviews, etc.

6. **Identifying and Documenting the Data Gaps:**
   a. <u>Identify data gaps</u> that affect the ability to identify conditions indicative of releases or threatened releases of hazardous substances on, at, in or to the subject property.
   b. <u>Comment</u> regarding the significance of the data gaps with regard to the ability to identify conditions indicative of releases or threatened releases of hazardous substances.
   c. <u>Comment</u> regarding the significance of the data gaps on the Environmental Professional's ability to provide an opinion as to whether the "All Appropriate Inquiries" have identified conditions indicative of releases or threatened releases.
   d. <u>Identify the sources of information consulted to address</u>, or fill, such data gaps.

   ". . . [T]he final regulation . . . requires that environmental professionals document and comment on the significance of only those data gaps that 'affect the ability of the environmental professional to identify conditions indicative of releases or threatened releases of hazardous substances *** on, at, in, or to the subject property.' If certain information included within the objectives and performance factors for the final rule cannot be found and the lack of certain information, in light of all other information that was collected about the property, has no bearing on the environmental professional's ability to render an opinion regarding the environmental conditions at the property, the final rule does not require the lack of such information to be documented in the final report." (AAI Final Rule, Section IV, N, pg. 66088.)

7. **Sampling and Analysis May Fill Data Gaps:** *"Section 312.20(g) of the final rule points out that one way to address data gaps may be to conduct sampling and analysis. The final regulation does not require that sampling and analysis be conducted to comply with the all appropriate inquiries requirements. The regulation only notes that sampling and analysis may be conducted, where appropriate, to obtain information to address data gaps. The Agency notes that sampling and analysis may be valuable in determining the possible presence and extent of potential contamination at a property. Such information may be valuable for determining how a landowner may best fulfill his or her post-acquisition continuing obligations required under the statute for obtaining protection from CERCLA liability."* (AAI Final Rule, Section IV, N, pg. 66089.)

8. **Data Gaps Do Not Necessarily Affect AAI Liability Protection:** *"If a person properly conducts all appropriate inquiries pursuant to this rule, including the requirements concerning data gaps at § 312.10, 312.20(g), and 312.21(c)(2), <u>the person may fulfill the all appropriate inquiries requirements of CERCLA sections 107(q), 107(r), and 101(35), even when there are data gaps in the inquiries</u>."* (AAI Final Rule, Section IV, N, pg. 66088-89, underlining added.)

9. **Data Gaps Do Not Negate Continuing Obligations:** Even though a person may fulfill the "All Appropriate Inquiries" requirements (and receive the protections), even when there are data gaps, that does not diminish post-acquisition Continuing Obligations.
   "The failure to detect a release during the conduct of all appropriate inquiries does not exempt a landowner from his or her post-acquisition continuing obligations under other provisions of the statute." (AAI Final Rule, Section IV, N, pg. 66089.)

[Ref: AAI Final Rule, Subpart C—Standards and Practices; § 312.20 "All Appropriate Inquiries" (g), pg. 66109-10.]

Z. What Is the Standard of Care?

In addition to issues regarding "How Much Research Is Enough" (See X:), "Data Gaps" (See Y:), "Professional Judgment" (See V:) and "Performance Factors" (See W:), there are a number of other factors to consider as to the standard of care in any particular situation.

1. **AAI Limited to CERCLA Landowner Liability Protection:** The AAI Final Rule is specifically intended to define the requirements necessary to obtain CERCLA landowner liability protections.

2. **ASTM—Not Necessarily the Standard of Care:** ASTM sets limits as to the applicability and use of the revised Phase I. ASTM indicates (both in its earlier version and in the E1527-05 version) that:
    "This practice offers a set of instructions for performing one or more specific operations. This document cannot replace education or experience and should be used in conjunction with professional judgment. Not all aspects of this practice may be applicable in all circumstances. This ASTM standard practice is not intended to represent or replace the standard of care by which the adequacy of a given professional service must be judged, nor should this document be applied without consideration of a project's many unique aspects. The word 'Standard' in the title means only that the document has been approved through the ASTM consensus process." (ASTM Phase I, E1527-05, Section 1.6, underlining added.)

3. **ASTM—Other Avenues for Good Commercial Practice:** ASTM additionally indicates that its Phase I Standard Practice is not necessarily the only road to fulfilling good commercial practice:
    "This practice is intended for use on a voluntary basis . . . . This practice is intended primarily as an approach to conducting an inquiry designed to identify recognized environmental conditions in connection with a property. No implication is intended that a person must use this practice in order to be deemed to have conducted inquiry in a commercially prudent or reasonable manner in any particular transaction. Nevertheless, this practice is intended to reflect a commercially prudent and reasonable inquiry."
    (ASTM Phase I, E1527-05, Section 4.1, underlining added.)

4. **ASTM—Comparison with Subsequent Inquiry:** *"It should not be concluded or assumed that an inquiry was not 'all appropriate inquiry' merely because the inquiry did not identify recognized environmental conditions in connection with a property. Environmental site assessments must be evaluated based on the reasonableness of judgments made at the time and under the circumstances in which they were made. Subsequent environmental site assessments should not be considered valid standards to judge the appropriateness of any prior assessment based on hindsight, new information, use of developing technology or analytical techniques or other factors."*
    (ASTM Phase I, E1527-05, Section 4.5.4.)

5. **ASTM—Prior Standards:** Some persons or institutions (reportedly even lenders) that do not see the need for a "higher" standard may wish to use the prior ASTM Phase I documents (E1527-00, etc.). However, the E1527-00 is now withdrawn and archived (certainly after November 1, 2006). Thus, an intent to comply with a prior ASTM Phase I may be problematic.

6. **ASTM—Business Environmental Risk:** The ASTM Phase I does not, per se, include business environmental risk evaluation.
    ". . . [A]n evaluation of business environmental risk associated with a parcel of commercial real estate may necessitate investigation beyond that identified in this practice."
    (ASTM Phase I, E1527-05, Section 1.1. See also Sections 1.3 and 4.4.)

However, ASTM provides for consideration of issues that go beyond addressing CERCLA liability concerns (ASTM Phase I, E1527-05, Section 1.1, 1.3). These are known as "Additional Services" (see ASTM Phase I, E1527-05, Section 12.9) and/or "Non-Scope Considerations" (see ASTM Phase I, E1527-05, Section 13). Such additional non-scope services can include asbestos, radon, lead in drinking water, lead-based paint, mold, etc.

7. **ASTM—Does Not Address Continuing Obligations:** The revised ASTM Phase I does not address Continuing Obligations. (See also Part IX: Continuing Obligations.)

8. **Licensed vs. Non-Licensed Environmental Professionals:** AAI (and ASTM) permits various persons to be "Environmental Professionals." These include state licensed professionals (P.E.s, P.G.s and others) as well as non-licensed persons. State licensed professionals may have differing responsibilities under state statutes compared to non-licensed individuals (e.g., regarding the protection of human health, safety and the environment).

9. **ASTM—Common Consultant Practice:** There is little hard data available regarding the specific degree to which Environmental Professionals use the ASTM Phase I Standard Practice. However, the most common opinion is that most Environmental Professionals do not strictly follow the ASTM Phase I Standard Practice. In fact, many knowledgeable persons believe that no more than perhaps five to ten percent (5-10%) of Environmental Professionals attempt to strictly follow the ASTM Phase I Standard Practice. (This does not diminish the importance or value of the ASTM Phase I. It merely acknowledges that as good of a "consensus road map" as it may be, different circumstances and professional judgments ultimately lead to variations in practice.)

10. **Local Custom:** The standard of care may be influenced by local custom.

11. **Contractual Arrangements:** Particular work scopes between Environmental Professionals and clients (users) vary. Issues regarding additional investigations, Phase II sampling and analysis and Continuing Obligations are subject to broad variability in contractual arrangements.

12. **ASTM—User Not Interested in AAI:** The ASTM Phase I is equally applicable to users who are not qualified for, or interested in, the "All Appropriate Inquiries" landowner liability benefits. These may include (a) lenders, (b) lessees, (c) refinancing situations, etc.

13. **User Risk Comfort Level:** The risk comfort level of the user (client) influences the standard of care. Environmental Professionals have a variety of relationships that necessitate varying considerations.

14. **Intended Use of Property:** The intended use of the property may influence the standard of care. For example, is the property to be used for a warehouse or a school?

15. **Weight of Evidence:** Regarding "how much research is enough" (as well as regarding additional investigations and/or Phase II sampling and analysis), CERLCA liability defenses require a "preponderance of the evidence," i.e., that something is more probable than not.

PART IV: "ALL APPROPRIATE INQUIRIES" FRAMEWORK

AA. Scope and Objectives of the AAI Site Assessment

1. **Scope:** *"The scope of the inquiries is to identify releases and threatened releases of hazardous substances which cause or threaten to cause the incurrence of response costs."* (AAI Final Rule, Section IV, A, pg. 66076.)

2. **Objective:** *"The primary objectives of the U.S. EPA's AAI Final Rule are to <u>identify the following types of information</u> about the subject property prior to acquiring the property . . . and which is intended to characterize the environmental conditions at the property that are indicative of releases or threatened releases of hazardous substances on, at, in, or to the subject property:*
   a. *Current and past property uses and occupancies;*
   b. *Current and past uses of hazardous substances;*
   c. *Waste management and disposal activities that could have caused releases or threatened releases of hazardous substances;*
   d. *Current and past corrective actions and response activities undertaken to address past and ongoing releases of hazardous substances;*
   e. *Engineering controls;*
   f. *Institutional controls; and*
   g. *Properties adjoining or located nearby the subject property that have environmental conditions that could have resulted in conditions indicative of releases or threatened releases of hazardous substances (on, at, in, or) to the subject property."*
   (AAI Final Rule, Subpart C—Standards and Practices, § 312.20 "All Appropriate Inquiries" (e)(1), pg. 66109; and Section IV, L, pg. 66087.)

Note: Although the statute speaks of *"all appropriate inquiries into the previous <u>ownership and uses</u> of the property"* (underlining added), the AAI Final Rule focuses on uses and activities at the property. (See also Part HH: Historical Sources of Information.)

BB. U.S. EPA Brownfields Grantees

For U.S. EPA Brownfields Grantees (Brownfields Assessment and Characterization Grants awarded under CERLCA Section 104(k)(2)(B)), the definition of "hazardous substances" is broadened (as per the terms and conditions of the grant) to go beyond the CERCLA definition of hazardous substances (CERLCA Section 101(22)) and also includes *pollutants and contaminants* (CERCLA Section 101(33)), *petroleum and petroleum products* (CERCLA Section 101(14)) *and controlled substances* (as defined in 21 U.S.C. 802).

[Ref: AAI Final Rule, Subpart C—Standards and Practices, § 312.20 "All Appropriate Inquiries" (e)(2), pg. 66109; and Section IV, A, pg. 66076.]

CC. Components of the "All Appropriate Inquiries" Assessment

1. **Inquiry must be done by an Environmental Professional** (40 CFR Parts 312.10 and 312.21).

2. **Components Which Are the Responsibility of the Environmental Professional:**
   a. Interview past and present owners, operators and occupants of the facility for the purpose of gathering information regarding the potential for contamination at the facility (40 CFR Part 312.23).
   b. Review historical sources of information such as (but not limited to) chain of title documents, aerial photographs, building department records and land use records, to determine previous uses and occupancies of the real property since the property was first developed (40 CFR Part 312.24).
   c. Review Federal, Tribal, State and Local government records, waste disposal records, underground storage tank records and hazardous waste handling, generation, treatment, disposal and spill records, concerning contamination at or near the facility (40 CFR Part 312.26).
   d. Visually inspect the subject property and adjoining properties (40 CFR Part 312.27).
   e. Include the degree of obviousness of the presence or likely presence of contamination at the property, and the ability to detect the contamination by appropriate investigation (40 CFR Part 312.31).
   Note: Although this item is primarily the obligation of the Environmental Professional, the prospective landowner (or Grantee) also shares this requirement (see § 312.31, pg. 66112).

3. **Components ("Additional Inquiries") Which Are the Responsibility of the Prospective Landowner (Buyer or Grantee) and Which Should Be Provided to the Environmental Professional:**
   a. Include any specialized knowledge or experience on the part of the prospective landowner (CERCLA defendant) or Grantee (40 CFR Part 312.28).
   Note: Regarding the specialized knowledge or experience on the part of the prospective landowner (or Grantee), see also Part DD: Prospective Landowner (Buyer) Should Conduct the AAI/Phase I.
   b. Include the relationship of purchase price to the fair market value of the subject property if the property was not contaminated (40 CFR Part 312.29).

4. **Components ("Additional Inquiries") Which Are the Responsibility of Either the Prospective Landowner (Buyer or Grantee) or the Environmental Professional:**
   a. Search for recorded environmental cleanup liens against the subject property that are filed or recorded under federal, tribal, state or local law (40 CFR Part 312.25). This item may be obtained by the prospective landowner or the Environmental Professional, or by a title search company or other third party.

5. **Components ("Additional Inquiries") Which Are the Responsibility of Both the Environmental Professional and the Prospective Landowner (Buyer or Grantee):** Include commonly known or reasonably ascertainable information about the property (40 CFR Part 312.30). See also 2(c) above.

Note 1: Additional Inquiries—Four of the above "All Appropriate Inquiries" components are designated in the Final Rule as "Additional Inquiries." These four components are (a) specialized knowledge or experience of the prospective landowner or grantee; (b) relationship of the purchase price to the fair market value if not contaminated; (c) environmental cleanup liens; and (d) commonly known or reasonably ascertainable information (see § 312.22, pg. 66110).

These "Additional Inquiries" are specifically the obligation of the prospective landowner (or Grantee) and not of the Environmental Professional. However, the "Additional Inquiries" may be fulfilled by others on behalf of the prospective landowner.
   "We also defined 'additional inquiries' that must be conducted by the prospective landowner or grantee (or an individual on the prospective landowner's or grantee's behalf)."
   (AAI Final Rule, Section III, Summary of Comments and Changes from Proposed to Final Rule, pg. 66076.)

The requirements for "relationship of the purchase price to the fair market value . . .," "environmental cleanup liens . . ." and "commonly known information . . ." may somewhat easily be fulfilled by another person (including the Environmental Professional) on behalf of the prospective landowner. However, it is less clear how the requirement regarding "specialized knowledge or experience of the prospective landowner or grantee" can be fulfilled by another person on behalf of the prospective landowner. In particular, the prospective landowner certainly would not be entitled not to disclose his/her actual knowledge regarding the property.

Note 2: <u>User Questionnaire</u>—ASTM provides a "User Questionnaire" which the User must answer. It is designed to address the above four requirements of the prospective landowner (as well as information regarding Activity and Use Limitations and Environmental Liens). The User Questionnaire is found at Appendix X3 of the ASTM Phase I.

Note 3: <u>User's Employees</u>—The AAI Final Rule does not specifically address any requirement regarding employees, subcontractors or others affiliated with the prospective landowner.

6. **ASTM—Components of the Phase I:** The revised ASTM Phase I maintains the principal components of an environmental site assessment as follows:

> *A Phase I Environmental Site Assessment shall have four components:*
> *7.2.1 Records Review*
> *7.2.2 Site Reconnaissance*
> *7.2.3 Interviews*
> *7.2.4 Report*

Note: ASTM refers to federal, state, tribal and local government records as "Environmental Information." ASTM refers to historical sources of information as "Historical Use Information." ASTM then put both these categories under one umbrella term called "Records Review."

[Ref: AAI Final Rule, Subpart C—Standards and Practices § 312.20 "All Appropriate Inquiries," pg. 66108-09, and § 312.22 "Additional Inquiries," pg. 66110; and Section IV, G, pg. 66081; also see CERCLA Section 101(35)(2)(B)(iii).]

DD. <u>Prospective Landowner (Buyer) Should Conduct the AAI/Phase I</u>

1. **Prospective Landowner Is Responsible Party:** In order to receive the "All Appropriate Inquiries" liability protections, the prospective landowner (Buyer—not Seller) is the responsible party to conduct the AAI. The law specifically states that it is the person claiming any of the landowner protections who must do the inquiries. This is repeated in the AAI Final Rule:

   ". . . inquiries must be conducted by persons seeking any of the landowner liability protections under CERCLA prior to acquiring a property." (AAI Final Rule, Section IV, A, pg. 66076.)

   "The Brownfields Amendments to CERCLA require persons claiming any of the landowner liability protections to conduct all appropriate inquiries into the past uses and ownership of the subject property." (AAI Final Rule, Section IV, H, pg. 66082.)

2. **Third Party AAI Not Sufficient:** The AAI Final Rule does not consider the use of a third party's (e.g., seller's) AAI/Phase I alone as being sufficient for achieving liability protection:

   ". . . it is not sufficient to wholly adopt previously conducted all appropriate inquiries for the same property without any review. Certain aspects of the all appropriate inquiries investigation are specific to the current prospective landowner and the current purchase transaction. . . ." (AAI Final Rule, Section IV, J, pg. 66084.)

   "Some of the statutory criteria are inherently the responsibility of the prospective landowner." (AAI Final Rule, Section IV, H, pg. 66082.)

   "All appropriate inquiries, as outlined in § 312.20, are not complete unless the results of the inquiries take into account the relevant and applicable specialized knowledge and experience of the persons responsible for undertaking the inquiry [prospective landowners or grantees]." (AAI Final Rule, Subpart C—Standards and Practices, § 312.28 "Specialized Knowledge or Experience on the Part of the Defendant" (b), pg. 66112.)

   "Throughout the inquiries, persons to whom this part is applicable per § 312.1(b) [prospective landowners and Grantees] and environmental professionals conducting the inquiry must take into account. . . ." (AAI Final Rule, Subpart C—Standards and Practices, § 312.30 "Commonly Known or Reasonably Ascertainable Information" (a), pg. 66112.)

3. **Using a Seller's Report:** However, the AAI Final Rule allows the purchaser to use a report conducted by another party (e.g., a seller) provided that:
   a. the purchaser determines that the report meets the objectives and performance factors and is in compliance with the AAI Final Rule;
   b. the purchaser reviews all the information collected and updates as necessary;
   c. the purchaser conducts additional inquiries regarding relevant specialized knowledge held by the purchaser, the relationship of purchase price to value of the property if the property was not contaminated, and commonly known or reasonably ascertainable information; and
   d. if the report conducted by the other party was done more than 180 days prior to prospective landowner acquisition of the property, then additional items would also have to be redone.
   (See AAA: Time Constraints (Shelf Life).)

[Ref: AAI Final Rule, Subpart C—Standards and Practices, § 312.20 "All Appropriate Inquiries" (d), pg. 66109.]

Note: Although the above parameters allow a buyer to use a report provided by a seller, it also exposes the "All Appropriate Inquiries" process to questions that could conceivably jeopardize the credibility of the report for AAI landowner liability defenses. For example, in the event of a complication at a later time, it might be rather easy to question whether, in fact, the report prepared for the seller actually met the objectives and performance factors of the AAI Final Rule.

A "Reliance Letter," "Certification to Buyer," "Assignment," "Reissuance" or other such device which simply relies on the seller's AAI/Phase I may jeopardize the liability protection available to the buyer (unless the above additional steps are undertaken).

Furthermore, buyers and sellers may not share the same environmental documentation objectives any longer. A seller, for example, may prefer to minimize documentation of possible contamination, while a buyer may want more detailed documentation in order to receive the AAI protections.

Considering all the above, it is clearly preferable for the buyer to conduct the AAI, and not rely on seller or other third party assessments.

See also Part TT: Specialized Knowledge of the Prospective Landowner, and UU: Relationship of Purchaser Price to Value.

[Ref: AAI Final Rule, Sections IV, H, I, J, K, pg. 66082-85.]

EE. "De Minimis" Contamination

1. **De Minimis Exclusion:** The AAI Final Rule excludes from the scope of the environmental inquiry any quantities or amounts of hazardous substances that would not pose a threat to human health or the environment.

   "These standards and practices however are not intended to require the identification in the written report prepared pursuant to § 312.21(c) of quantities or amounts, either individually or in the aggregate, of hazardous substances, pollutants, contaminants, petroleum and petroleum products, and controlled substances (as defined in 21 U.S.C. 802) that because of said quantities and amounts, generally would not pose a threat to human health or the environment."
   (AAI Final Rule, Subpart C—Standards and Practices, § 312.20(h), pg. 66110.)

   "The final (rule) retains the provision that the environmental professional need not specifically identify, in the written report prepared pursuant to § 312.21(c), extremely small quantities or amounts of contaminants, so long as the contaminants generally would not pose a threat to human health or the environment." (AAI Final Rule, Section IV, O, pg. 66089.)

2. **ASTM—De Minimis Exclusion:** Because the Final Rule Preamble uses the phrase "extremely small quantities," this can be termed "De Micromis" contamination. However, ASTM uses the "De minimis" description.

   "The term [Recognized Environmental Conditions] is not intended to include de minimis conditions that generally do not present a threat to human health or the environment and that generally would not be the subject of an enforcement action if brought to the attention of appropriate governmental agencies." (ASTM Phase I, E1527-05, Section 1.1.1.)

FF. Interim Standards

The law provides interim "All Appropriate Inquiries" standards for commercial/industrial properties purchased prior to the effective date of the AAI Final Rule.

1. **Prior to May 31, 1997:** For properties purchased prior to May 31, 1997, the standard is the basic language relating to the CERCLA third party defense that:
    > *"persons . . . must demonstrate that they carried out all appropriate inquiries into the previous ownership and uses of the property in accordance with generally accepted good commercial and customary standards and practices."*

    This includes the following five elements:
    i.)   any specialized knowledge or experience on the part of the defendant;
    ii.)   the relationship of the purchase price to the value of the property if the property were not contaminated;
    iii.) commonly known or reasonably ascertainable information about the property;
    iv.)   the obviousness of the presence or likely presence of contamination at the property; and
    v.)   the ability of the defendant to detect the contamination by appropriate inspection.
    (See ASTM Phase I, E1527-05, Appendix 1.3.3.)

    Note: Properties purchased prior to May 31, 1997, can only be eligible for the Innocent Landowner defense or the Contiguous Property Owner protection.

2. **Prior to November 1, 2005:** For properties purchased on or after May 31, 1997, but before November 1, 2005, the interim standard is ASTM E1527-97 or ASTM E1527-00.

    Note: The Bona Fide Prospective Purchaser protection was only effective as of January 11, 2002.

3. **Prior to November 1, 2006:** For properties purchased on or after November 1, 2005, but before November 1, 2006, the interim standard is ASTM E1527-97 or ASTM E1527-00 or ASTM E1527-05.

4. **November 1, 2006:** As of November 1, 2006, when all the interim standards are no longer operative, the only acceptable standard is the AAI Final Rule and, optionally, the ASTM E1527-05 (if conducted per the AAI Final Rule requirements).

[Ref: AAI Final Rule, Section II, C, pg. 66072.]

GG. Residential Standard

1. **Definition of "Residential":** The residential landowner liability protection standard applies to properties acquired by a nongovernmental entity or noncommercial entity for residential or other similar uses.

2. **Standard for Landowner Liability Protections:** For residential properties (not purchased for nonresidential purposes), the "All Appropriate Inquiries" standard consists of a:
    > *"Facility inspection and title search that reveal no basis for further investigation."*

3. **No AAI Requirement:** Other than this standard, residential properties are not within the scope of the "All Appropriate Inquiries" Rule.

4. **Final Standard:** This residential standard has no date restrictions and is not merely an interim standard.

[Ref: AAI Final Rule, Section II, C, pg. 66072.]

PART V: HISTORICAL & RECORDS RESEARCH REQUIREMENTS

Note: ASTM refers to federal, state, tribal and local government records as "Environmental Information." ASTM refers to historical sources of information as "Historical Use Information." ASTM then put both these categories under one umbrella term called "Records Review."

HH. Historical Sources of Information

1. **Requirement For Historical Research:** The statutory criteria and the "All Appropriate Inquiries" Final Rule mandate the need to research historical sources of information.
    > *"Historical documents and records must be reviewed for the purposes of achieving the objectives and performance factors. . . ."* (AAI Final Rule, Subpart C—Standards and Practices, § 312.24 "Reviews of Historical Sources of Information" (a), pg. 66111.)

2. **No Specific Lists:** The AAI Final Rule does not prescribe a specific list of historical sources, and additionally indicates that there is no requirement to utilize any particular type of historical source(s).
    > *"The final rule does not require that any specific type of historic information be collected."*
    > (AAI Final Rule, Section IV, Q, pg. 66091.)

3. **No Chain of Title Required:** The AAI Final Rule not only does not prescribe a specific list of historical sources but it also specifically indicates that when researching historical sources, there is no particular requirement to research chain of title.
    > *"In particular, the rule does not require that persons obtain a chain of title document for the property."*
    > (AAI Final Rule, Section IV, Q, pg. 66091.)

    Note: Some persons question this provision. The statute itself requires *"all appropriate inquiries into the previous ownership and uses of the property. . . ."* How does one obtain previous ownership without a chain of title?

    However, despite the language in the statute, the AAI Final Rule and the ASTM Phase I do not focus on ownership, but only on property uses and occupancies. The AAI Final Rule and the ASTM Phase I both allow for the use of a chain of title in developing a history of previous uses, but neither require a chain of title.

    The common standard of practice appears to be not to expect a chain of title in an AAI/Phase I.

4. **Examples of Historical Sources:** The AAI Final Rule offers examples of historical sources. Historical documents and records may include (but not limited to) aerial photographs, fire insurance maps, building department records, chain of title documents and land use records to determine previous uses and occupancies of the real property.

5. **Surrounding Uses:** The AAI Final Rule includes a specific objective to identify *"properties adjoining or located nearby the subject property that have environmental conditions that could have resulted in conditions indicative of releases or threatened releases of hazardous substances (on, at, in, or) to the subject property."* (AAI Final Rule, Subpart C—Standards and Practices, § 312.20 "All Appropriate Inquiries" (e)(1)(vii), pg. 66109; and Section IV, L, pg. 66087.)

    This applies to the requirement that government records be searched for the surrounding area. However, as to what historical sources may also need to be researched, if any, regarding nearby properties, this is left to the professional judgment of the Environmental Professional.

6. **Previously Collected Information & Secondary Sources:** The AAI Final Rule specifically permits the use of previously collected information and secondary sources:

    ". . . the prospective landowner, grantee, or environmental professional may make use of previously collected information about a property when conducting all appropriate inquiries. The collection of historical information about a property may be a particular case where previously collected information may be valuable, as well as easily accessible. In addition, nothing in the rule prohibits a person from using secondary sources (e.g., a previously conducted title search) when gathering information about historical ownership and usage of a property . . . information must be updated if it was last collected more than 180 days prior to the date of acquisition of the property." (AAI Final Rule, Section IV, Q, pg. 66092.)

    ASTM has a similar provision (see ASTM Phase I, E1527-05, Section 8.4).

7. **Performance Factors:** This is subject to the performance factor provision that the Environmental Professional *"gather the information . . . that is publicly available, obtainable from its source within reasonable time and cost restraints, and which can practically be reviewed."* (AAI Final Rule, Subpart C—Standards and Practices, § 312.20 "All Appropriate Inquiries" (f), pg. 66109. See also Part W: Performance Factors.)

8. **ASTM—"Standard Historical Sources":** ASTM provides a specific list of eight "Standard Historical Sources." (ASTM Phase I, E1527-05, Section 8.3.4.)

    The eight (8) ASTM Standard Historical Sources are:
    * Aerial Photographs
    * Fire Insurance Maps (e.g., Sanborn, Hopkins, etc.)
    * Property Tax Files (e.g., past ownership, appraisals, maps, sketches, photos)
    * Recorded Land Title Records*
    * USGS Topographic Maps (7.5 minute topo maps preferred)
    * Local Street Directories (e.g., Criss-Cross Directories)
    * Building Department Records
    * Zoning/Land Use Records

    *Notes regarding recorded land title records:
    "Information about the title to the property that is recorded in a U.S. district court or any place other than where land title records are, by law or custom, recorded for the local jurisdiction in which the property is located, are not considered part of recorded land title records. . . ."
    "[Recorded land title records] cannot be the sole historical source consulted. If this source is consulted, at least one additional standard historical source must also be consulted."
    (ASTM Phase I, E1527-05, Section 8.3.4.4.)

9. **ASTM—How Many "Standard Historical Sources" Must Be Reviewed:** *"Uses of the property—. . . This task requires reviewing only as many of the standard historical sources . . . as are necessary and both reasonably ascertainable and likely to be useful. . . ."* (ASTM Phase I, E1527-05, Section 8.3.2.)

10. **ASTM—Descriptions of Types of Uses:** *". . . it is sufficient . . . to identify the general type of use (for example: office, retail and residential) unless it is obvious from the source(s) consulted that the use may be more specifically identified. However, if the general type of use is industrial or manufacturing (for example, zoning/land use records show industrial zoning), then additional standard historical sources should be reviewed if they are likely to identify a more specific use and are reasonably ascertainable."* (ASTM Phase I, E1527-05, Section 8.3.2.2.)

11. **ASTM—"Obvious" Uses:** *"All <u>obvious</u> uses of the property shall be identified from the present, back to the property's first developed use, or back to 1940, whichever is earlier."* (ASTM Phase I, E1527-05, Section 8.3.2, underlining added.)

Note: The prior ASTM Phase I Standard Practice (E1527-00) had the following requirement: *"All <u>obvious</u> uses of the property shall be identified from the present, back to the property's <u>obvious</u> first developed use, or back to 1940, whichever is earlier."* (ASTM Phase I, E1527-00, Section 7.3.2, underlining added.)

12. **ASTM—Performance Factors Regarding "Standard Historical Sources":**
"Uses of the property—it would not be required to review them [standard sources of information regarding uses of the property] *unless they were both reasonably ascertainable and likely to be useful. . . ."* (ASTM Phase I, E1527-05, Section 8.3.2.)

"Data Failure—. . . Data failure occurs when all of the standard historical sources that are reasonably ascertainable and likely to be useful have been reviewed and yet the objectives have not been met. Data failure is not uncommon. . . ." (ASTM Phase I, E1527-05, Section 8.3.2.3.)

"Notwithstanding a data failure, standard historical sources may be excluded if: (1) the sources are not reasonably ascertainable, or (2) if past experience indicates that the sources are not likely to be sufficiently useful, accurate, or complete. . . ." (ASTM Phase I, E1527-05 Section 8.3.2.3.)

"Accuracy and completeness of record information varies among information sources, including government sources. Record information is often inaccurate or incomplete. The user or Environmental Professional is not obligated to identify mistakes or insufficiencies in information provided." (ASTM Phase I, E1527-05, Section 8.1.3.)

13. **ASTM—"Other Historical Sources" Not Required:** These include historical sources which are not included within the list of "standard historical sources," e.g., miscellaneous maps, newspaper archives, Internet sites, community organizations, local libraries, historical societies, current owner or occupants of neighboring properties and records in the files and/or personal knowledge of the property owner and/or occupant. (ASTM Phase I, E1527-05, Section 3.2.58; 8.3.4.9.)
> *"Other historical sources specified in 8.3.4.9 may be used to satisfy the objectives, but are not required to comply with this practice."* (ASTM Phase I, E1527-05, Section 8.3.2.3.)

14. **ASTM—Surrounding Uses:**
"The objective of consulting historical sources is to develop a history of the previous uses of the property and surrounding area. . . ." (ASTM Phase I, E1527-05, Section 8.3.1.)

"Uses in the area surrounding the property shall be identified in the report, but this task is required only to the extent that this information is revealed in the course of researching the property itself. . . ."
(ASTM Phase I, E1527-05, Section 8.3.3.)

The Environmental Professional has discretionary judgment regarding identification of surrounding uses when using sources that include the surrounding area. (See Section 8.3.2.)

II. How Far Back?

1. **First Developed Use:** The AAI Final Rule requires that *"Historical documents and records reviewed must cover a period of time as far back in the history of the subject property as it can be shown that the property contained structures or from the time the property was first used for residential, agricultural, commercial, industrial, or governmental purposes."* (AAI Final Rule, Subpart C—Standards and Practices, § 312.24 "Reviews of Historical Sources of Information" (b), pg. 66111.)

2. **EP May Modify "How Far Back":** The AAI Final Rule states that *"the final rule does allow the environmental professional to exercise his or her professional judgment 'in context of the facts available at the time of the inquiry as to how far back in time it is necessary to search historical records.' We believe that this provides sufficient flexibility to allow for any circumstances where, due to the availability of other information about a property, an environmental professional may conclude that a comprehensive search of historical records is not necessary to meet the objectives and performance factors."* (AAI Final Rule, Section IV, Q, pg. 66091.)

3. **ASTM—First Developed Use or 1940:** ASTM always requires going back no less than to 1940. (If the property was first developed after 1940, the AAI requirement would only go back to that first developed use.)

4. **ASTM—EP May Modify "How Far Back":** *"This task requires reviewing only as many of the standard historical sources . . . as are necessary and both reasonably ascertainable and likely to be useful . . . it would not be required to review them unless they were both reasonably ascertainable and likely to be useful."* (ASTM Phase I, E1527-05, Section 8.3.2.)

5. **ASTM—Presumptive Search Intervals:** ASTM has permitted, and continues to permit, a presumptive search interval of five years, unless uncovered data suggests the need for greater frequency.

JJ. Government Records Searches for the Subject Property

Note: The previous two sections related to historical sources (ASTM—"Historical Use Information"). The following sections relate to government records searches (ASTM—"Environmental Information").

1. **Required Records Searches:** *"With regard to the subject property, the review of federal, tribal and state government records or databases of such government records and local government records and databases of such records should include:*
    (1) Records of reported releases or threatened releases, including site investigation reports for the subject property;
    (2) Records of activities, conditions, or incidents likely to cause or contribute to releases or threatened releases as defined in § 312.1(c), including landfill and other disposal unit location records and permits, storage tank records and permits, hazardous waste handler and generator records and permits, federal, tribal and state government listings of sites identified as priority cleanup sites, and spill reporting records;
    (3) CERCLIS records—(EPA's Comprehensive Environmental Response, Compensation and Liability Information System database . . . including sites listed on the National Priorities List (NPL) . . . CERCLIS also contains information on sites being assessed under the Superfund program, hazardous waste sites and potential hazardous waste sites);
    (4) Public health records (Government-maintained records of public risks . . . available records documenting public health threats or concerns caused by, or related to, activities currently or previously conducted at the site);
    (5) Emergency Response Notification System (ERNS) records (EPA's database of oil and hazardous substance spill reports);
    (6) Registries or publicly available lists of engineering controls; and
    (7) Registries or publicly available lists of institutional controls, including environmental land use restrictions, applicable to the subject property."
    (AAI Final Rule, Subpart C—Standards and Practices, § 312.26 "Reviews of Federal, State, Tribal and Local Government Records" (b), pg. 66111; and Section IV, S, pg. 66094.)

2. **Databases Are Sufficient:** The requirements of the AAI Final Rule regarding government records may be met by searching databases which compile and contain these government records. A review of the actual government records themselves is not necessary.
    "The review of actual records is not necessary, provided that the same information contained in the government records and required to meet the requirements of this criterion and achieve the objectives and performance factors for these regulations is attainable by searching available databases."
    (AAI Final Rule, Section IV, S, pg. 66094-95.)

3. **ASTM—No Compliance Audits:**
    "Environmental compliance audits—The investigative process to determine if the operations of an existing facility are in compliance with applicable environmental laws and regulations. This term should not be used to describe this practice. . . ." (ASTM Phase I, E1527-05, Section 3.2.27.)

    "This practice does not address requirements of any state or local laws or of any federal laws other than the all appropriate inquiry provisions of the LLPs [landowner liability protections]. . . ."
    (ASTM Phase I, E1527-05, Section 1.1.4.)

[Ref: AAI Final Rule, Subpart C—Standards and Practices, § 312.26 "Reviews of Federal, State, Tribal and Local Government Records, pg. 66111.]

KK. Government Records Searches for Adjoining and Neighboring Properties

1. **Required Records Searches:** The AAI Final Rule also requires that government records for adjoining and nearby properties be reviewed to assess the potential impact to the subject property from hazardous substances migrating from adjoining or nearby properties that could result in conditions indicative of releases or threatened releases of hazardous substances to the subject property.

   "With regard to nearby or adjoining properties, the review of federal, tribal, state and local government records or databases of government records should include the identification of the following:

   (1) Properties for which there are government records of reported releases or threatened releases . . .
   - *i.   records of NPL sites or tribal and state-equivalent sites (1 mile),*
   - *ii. RCRA facilities subject to corrective action (1 mile),*
   - *iii. records of federally-registered, or state-permitted or registered, hazardous waste sites identified for investigation or remediation, such as sites enrolled in state and tribal voluntary cleanup programs and tribal and state-listed Brownfields sites (½ mile),*
   - *iv. records of leaking underground storage tanks (½ mile);*

   (2) Properties that previously were identified or regulated by a government entity due to environmental conditions at the property . . .
   - *i.   Records of delisted NPL sites (½ mile);*
   - *ii. Registries or publicly available lists of engineering controls (½ mile); and*
   - *iii. Records of former CERLCIS sites with no further remedial action notices (½ mile);*

   (3) Properties for which there are records of federally-permitted, tribal-permitted or registered, or state-permitted or registered waste management activities. . .
   - *i.   Records of RCRA small quantity and large quantity generators (adjoining properties);*
   - *ii. Records of federally-permitted, tribal-permitted, or state-permitted (or registered) landfills and solid waste management facilities (½ mile); and*
   - *iii. Records of registered storage tanks (adjoining properties).*

   (4) A review of additional government records with regard to [nearby or adjoining properties] . . . may be necessary in the judgment of the environmental professional for the purpose of achieving the objectives and performance factors. . . ."

   (AAI Final Rule, Subpart C—Standards and Practices, § 312.26 Reviews of Federal, State, Tribal and Local Government Records (c), pg. 66111. See also Section IV, S, pg. 66094-95.)

2. **AAI Anomaly Regarding Engineering Controls Search Distance:** The AAI Final Rule makes contradictory statements regarding the required search distance for engineering controls.

   In the Preamble, the AAI Final Rule clearly indicates the intent of the U.S. EPA that engineering controls be searched only at the subject property.

   "The final rule requires that government records and available lists for institutional and engineering controls be searched only for information on such controls at the subject property. All appropriate inquiries investigations do not have to include searches for institutional and engineering controls in place at nearby and adjoining properties." (AAI Final Rule, Section IV, S, pg. 66093.)

   However, in the actual rule, engineering controls are included within the requirements for nearby properties, and require government records searches for one-half mile. (See § 312.26, Review of Federal, State, Tribal and Local Government Records, pg. 66111.)

   It appears that the one-half mile requirement is an unintentional listing on the part of the U.S. EPA, which apparently will not be enforced.

   ASTM, for its part, requires that engineering controls be searched only for the subject property.

   Note: This would only have been an issue in those (approximately thirteen) states with meaningful engineering control registries.

3. **ASTM—Required Records Searches:** ASTM has modified its database and search distance requirements to comply with the AAI Final Rule.

4. **ASTM—Consolidated Government Environmental Records Search Lists (Including the Subject Property Plus the Surrounding Area):**

Standard Environmental Record Sources (where available):	*Approximate Minimum Search Distance miles (kilometres)*
Federal	
Federal NPL site list	*1.0 (1.6)*
Federal Delisted NPL site list	*0.5 (0.8)*
Federal CERCLIS list	*0.5 (0.8)*
Federal CERCLIS NFRAP site list	*0.5 (0.8)*
Federal RCRA CORRACTS facilities list	*1.0 (1.6)*
Federal RCA non-CORRACTS TSD facilities list	*0.5 (0.8)*
Federal RCRA generators list	*property & adjoining properties*
Federal institutional control/engineering control registries	*property only*
Federal ERNS list	*property only*
State	
State and tribal lists of hazardous waste sites identified for investigation or remediation :	
State- and tribal-equivalent NPL	*1.0 (1.6)*
State- and tribal-equivalent CERCLIS	*0.5 (0.8)*
State and tribal landfill and/or solid waste disposal site lists	*0.5 (0.8)*
State and tribal leaking storage tank lists	*0.5 (0.8)*
State and tribal registered storage tank lists	*property & adjoining properties*
State and tribal institutional control/engineering control registries	*property only*
State and tribal voluntary cleanup sites	*0.5 (0.8)*
State and tribal Brownfield sites	*0.5 (0.8)*

(ASTM Phase I, E1527-05, Section 8.2.1.)

Note: "Approximate minimum search distance" is measured from the nearest property boundary.

5. **EP May Modify Search Distances:** *"The search distance from the subject property boundary for reviewing government records or databases of government records . . . may be modified based upon the professional judgment of the environmental professional. The rationale for such modifications must be documented by the environmental professional. The environmental professional may consider one or more of the following factors in determining an alternate appropriate search distance:*
- *The nature and extent of a release;*
- *Geologic, hydrogeologic, or topographic conditions of the subject property and surrounding environment;*
- *Land use or development densities;*
- *The property type;*
- *Existing or past uses of surrounding properties;*
- *Potential migration pathways (e.g., groundwater flow direction, prevalent wind direction); or*
- *Other relevant factors."*

(AAI Final Rule, Subpart C—Standards and Practices, § 312.26 Reviews of Federal, State, Tribal and Local Government Records (c), pg. 66111. See also Section IV, S, pg. 66094-95.)

6. **ASTM—EP May Modify Search Distances:**
    "The approximate minimum search distance may be reduced . . . for any of these standard environmental record sources except the federal NPL site list and federal RCRA TSD list. . . ."

    "Factors to consider in adjusting the approximate minimum search distance include:
    (1) the density (for example, urban, rural, or suburban) . . . (2) the distance that the hazardous substances or petroleum products are likely to migrate . . . (3) the property type, (4) existing or past uses of surrounding properties, and (5) other reasonable factors." (ASTM Phase I, E1527-05, Sections 8.2.1 and 8.1.2.1.)

7. **ASTM—USGS 7.5 Minute Topographic Maps:** As a "Physical Setting Source," ASTM additionally requires that the USGS 7.5 Minute Topographic Map (or equivalent) be reviewed for the area on which the property is located. When warranted, other geologic, hydrogeologic, hydrologic, or topographic related physical setting sources shall be sought. (ASTM Phase I, E1527-05, Section 8.2.3.)

    These physical setting sources include:
    Mandatory Standard Physical Setting Sources
        USGS—Current 7.5 Minute Topographic Map (or equivalent)

    Discretionary and Non-Standard Physical Setting Sources
        USGS and/or State Geological Survey—Groundwater Maps
        USGS and/or State Geological Survey—Bedrock Geology Maps
        USGS and/or State Geological Survey—Surficial Geology Maps
        Soil Conservation Service—Soil Maps
        Other Physical Setting Sources that are reasonably credible
            (as well as reasonably ascertainable)
    (ASTM Phase I, E1527-05, Section 8.2.3.)

[Ref: AAI Final Rule, Subpart C—Standards and Practices, § 312.26, pg. 66111 and Section IV, S, pg. 66094-95.]

LL. Mandate Regarding Local Government Records

1. **Requirement for Local Government Records Searches:** The AAI Final Rule mandates the review of local government records to the extent that such records are reasonably ascertainable. The AAI Final Rule uses the language "_must be reviewed_" in relation to local records, just as for federal, tribal, or state records. (AAI Final Rule, Subpart C—Standards and Practices, § 312.26 Reviews of Federal, State, Tribal and Local Records (a), pg. 66111.)

2. **ASTM—Now Mandatory (But Subject to EP Discretion):** Under ASTM, review of local government records has previously not been mandatory. In the revised ASTM Phase I:
    > "_local records and/or additional state or tribal records shall be checked when, in the judgment of the environmental professional, such additional records (1) are reasonably ascertainable, (2) are sufficiently useful, accurate and complete . . . and (3) are generally obtained, pursuant to local good or customary practice. . . ._"
    (ASTM Phase I, E1527-05, Section 8.2.2.)

3. **ASTM—Local Records and Sources That May Be Useful:**

    Types of Records
    Local Brownfield Lists
    Local Lists of Landfill/Solid Waste Disposal Sites
    Local Lists of Hazardous Waste/Contaminated Sites
    Local Lists of Registered Storage Tanks
    Local Land Records (for activity and use limitations)
    Records of Emergency Release Reports (42 U.S.C. 11004)
    Records of Contaminated Public Wells

    Sources
    Department of Health/Environmental Division
    Fire Department
    Planning Department
    Building Permit/Inspection Department
    Local/Regional Pollution Control Agency
    Local/Regional Water Quality Agency
    Local Electric Utility Companies (for records relating to PCBs)

    (ASTM Phase I, E1527-05, Section 8.2.2.)

MM. Institutional & Engineering Controls (IC/EC)

1. **Definition of Institutional Controls:** Institutional controls (IC) are *"non-engineered (restrictive) instruments, such as administrative and legal controls, that help to minimize the potential for human exposure to contamination and/or protect the integrity of a remedy."* (AAI Final Rule, Subpart B—Definitions, § 312.10, pg. 66108.)

   Institutional controls limit land or resource use and provide information to modify behavior.
   "Institutional controls often must remain in place for an indefinite duration and, therefore, generally need to survive changes in property ownership (i.e., run with the land) to be legally and practically effective."
   (AAI Final Rule, Section IV, M, pg. 66087.)

2. **IC Terms and Examples:** Institutional Controls can include various environmental related land use or deed restrictions, restrictive covenants, environmental covenants, easements, etc. Zoning can also be an example of a potential Institutional Control. For example, a particularly useful Institutional Control could be a prohibition on drilling a drinking water well in a contaminated aquifer or disturbing contaminated soil.

   Differing terms are frequently utilized by government bodies for Institutional Controls. These may include Land Use Controls or LUCs, Land Use Restrictions or LURs (used for Brownfields), Environmental Use Restrictions, etc.

   Note 1: Example terms of state IC registries include Declaration of Environmental Use Restriction database (Arizona), list of "Deed Restrictions" (California), Environmental Real Covenants Lists (Colorado), Brownfields site lists (Indiana, Missouri, Pennsylvania).

   Note 2: ASTM defines institutional controls and engineering controls as being subsets of Activity and Use Limitations (AULs). (See ASTM Phase I, E1527-05, Sections 3.2.2, 3.2.26 and 3.2.42.)

3. **Requirement For IC/EC Searches:** Institutional Controls (IC) and Engineering Controls (EC) are required to be searched regarding the subject property.
   "(b) with regard to the subject property, the review of federal, tribal and state government records or databases of such government records and local government records and databases of such records should include. . . .
   (6) registries or publicly available lists of engineering controls; and
   (7) registries or publicly available lists of institutional controls, including environmental land use restrictions, applicable to the subject property."
   (AAI Final Rule, Subpart C—Standards and Practices, § 312.26 Reviews Federal, State, Tribal and Local Government Records (b), pg. 66111.)

4. **Specifically Required within Government Records Searches:** Although Institutional Controls and Engineering Controls may be identified through various means (e.g., title restrictions, interviews, etc.), there is a specific requirement in the AAI Final Rule to review federal, state, tribal and local government registries or publicly available lists for IC/EC. As such, an IC/EC search is included in the government records search.

   Note: Federal, state and tribal records searches for IC/EC, if available, would generally be provided by a records database firm. Local records, if available, would be part of a local records search.

5. **Where Else May Institutional Controls (IC) Be Searched:**
   a. As indicated above, there is a specific requirement to search for ICs in *"registries or publicly available lists of institutional controls, including environmental land use restrictions, applicable to the subject property"* (see above).
   b. There is also a more general AAI recommendation to search for ICs, but which allows for a variety of options as to where to search.

   > *"Those persons conducting all appropriate inquiries may identify institutional controls through several of the standards and practices set forth in this rule. As noted, implementation of institutional controls may be accomplished through the use of several administrative and legal mechanisms, such as zoning restrictions, building permit requirements, easements, covenants, etc. For example, an easement implementing an institutional control might be identified through the review of chain of title documents under § 312.24(a). Furthermore, interviews with past and present owners, operators, or occupants . . . and reviews of federal, tribal, state and local government records . . . may identify an institutional control or refer a person to the appropriate source to find an institutional control."* (AAI Final Rule, Section IV, M, pg. 66087.)

As such, in addition to reviews of federal, state, tribal and local government registries or publicly available lists, institutional controls may also be identified through:

   a. restrictions of record on the title, e.g., covenants and restrictions, restrictive covenants, deed restrictions, easements, or other recorded land title records, etc.
       [These may not be included in a "chain-of-title" but are usually included in a "title search"];
   b. reviews of other federal, tribal, state and local government types of records (besides registries or publicly available lists), including zoning restrictions, building permit requirements, excavation permits, well drilling prohibitions or other government orders or consent decrees;
   c. interviews with past and present owners, operators or occupants;
   d. risk assessment documents;
   e. remedy decision or design documents; and
   f. other activity and use controls designed to isolate contamination.

6. **Definition of Engineering Controls:** Engineering controls (EC) are physical or structural barriers that isolate contaminated areas.

7. **EC Examples:** Engineering control examples include:
   a. fences;
   b. soil barriers;
   c. soil caps overlying contamination;
   d. concrete or asphalt caps overlying contamination;
   e. water treatment systems;
   f. other physical barriers designed to isolate contamination.

8. **ASTM—Limited Requirement for IC/EC Searches:** ASTM requires IC/EC searches (a) within registries and publicly available lists, and (b) within recorded land title records. The Environmental Professional is responsible for the former, and the user is responsible for the latter. There is no mandatory additional ASTM requirement to search for IC/ECs anywhere else. However, ASTM provides an optional User Questionnaire that includes questions encompassing IC/EC.

As such:

a. ASTM requires that Federal and State Government Records Searches include institutional controls and engineering controls registries. (Once again, note that ASTM combines institutional controls and engineering controls into one category called "Activity and Use Limitations" (AULs).)

b. Other than Federal and State IC/EC registries, ASTM generally limits the required searches for recorded Activity and Use Limitations (AULs) to <u>recorded land title records</u>.

> *"Except to the extent that applicable federal, state, local or tribal statutes, or regulations specify any place other than recorded land title records for recording or filing environmental liens or activity and use limitations or specify records to be reviewed to identify the existence of such environmental liens or activity and use limitations, environmental liens or activity and use limitations that are recorded or filed any place other than recorded land title records are not considered to be reasonably ascertainable."* (ASTM Phase I, E1527-05, Section 6.2.1.)

> *"Information about the title to the property that is recorded in a U.S. district court or anyplace other than where land title records are, by law or custom, recorded for the local jurisdiction in which the property is located, are not considered part of recorded land title records."* (ASTM Phase I, E1527-05, Section 3.2.75. See also 8.3.4.4.)

Note: In any event, searches in various courts (e.g., Federal, Common Pleas, Probate, Bankruptcy) are commonly conducted as part of title searches by title companies before preparing a title commitment/policy.

9. **ASTM—Responsibility of User but May Be Done by Title Company:** Regarding recorded land title records, ASTM makes the searches for Activity and Use Limitations (AULs) the responsibility of the user, and not the Environmental Professional.

> *"Unless added by a change in the scope of work to be performed by the environmental professional, this practice does not impose on the environmental professional the responsibility to undertake a review of recorded land title records and judicial records for environmental liens or activity and use limitations. The user should either (1) engage a title company or title professional . . . or (2) negotiate such an engagement of a title company or title professional as an addition to the scope of work to be performed by the environmental professional."* (ASTM Phase I, E1527-05, Section 6.2.)

Note 1: The search by the title search company for institutional controls and other environmental restrictions of record on the title also includes environmental cleanup liens.

Note 2: Title insurance companies are exempted from certain environmental considerations at the property. While that should not stop a title search from identifying an environmental related land use control, it appears that in some situations, some title search companies may not include such information on account of the environmental exemption. Because some title companies may deemphasize the need to identify institutional controls relating to environmental issues, it is best to clarify this matter with the title search company. Alternately, there are document search and retrieval companies (not affiliated with title companies) that specialize in environmental title searches.

NN. Recorded Environmental Cleanup Liens

1. **Definition of Recorded Environmental Cleanup Liens:** *"For purposes of this rule, recorded environmental cleanup liens are encumbrances on property for the recovery of incurred cleanup costs on the part of a state* [or local], *tribal, or federal government agency or other third party."* (AAI Final Rule, Section IV, R, pg. 66092.)

2. **Requirement for Recorded Environmental Cleanup Liens Searches:** *"All appropriate inquiries must include a search for the existence of environmental cleanup liens against the subject property that are filed or recorded under federal, tribal, state or local law."* (AAI Final Rule, Subpart C—Standards and Practices, § 312.25(a), pg. 66111.)

3. **Where Must Environmental Cleanup Liens Be Searched:** *"Environmental cleanup liens may be recorded as part of the land title records or as part of other state or local government land or real estate records. Recorded environmental cleanup liens may be recorded in different places, depending upon the particular state and particular locality in which the property is located."* (AAI Final Rule, Section IV, R, pg. 66092.)

    Note: The general intent is to check in the usual place where such liens are normally filed.

4. **Only Recorded Liens:** Liens that are not recorded by government programs or agencies are not addressed by the language of the statute. (The statute speaks only of recorded liens.)

5. **User Is Responsible for Recorded Environmental Cleanup Liens:** If not otherwise obtained by the Environmental Professional, recorded environmental cleanup liens may (and preferably should) be provided to the Environmental Professional by the prospective landowner. (AAI Final Rule, Subpart C—Standards and Practices, § 312.25(b), pg. 66111 and Section IV, R, pg. 66092.)

6. **Data Gaps:** If information regarding recorded environmental cleanup liens is not provided to the EP, the EP should note the lack of such information as a data gap.
    "If such information is not provided to the environmental professional and the lack of such information affects the ability of the environmental professional to identify conditions indicative of releases or threatened releases of hazardous substances on, at, in, or to the property, the lack of information should be noted as a data gap. . . ." (AAI Final Rule, Section IV, R, pg. 66092.)

7. **May be Done By Title Company:** The search for environmental cleanup liens does not require the expertise of an Environmental Professional and is generally done by the title search company.
    ". . . [W]e believe that the decision of who conducts the search may be best left up to the judgment of the prospective landowner or grantee and environmental professional. The final rule provides in § 312.22 that the search for recorded environmental cleanup liens can fall outside the inquiries conducted by the environmental professional. The search for recorded environmental cleanup liens is not included as part of the requirements governing the results of an inquiry by an environmental professional. . . .

    With regard to commenters who requested that EPA provide guidance on where to search for environmental cleanup liens, we advise that prospective landowners and grantees seek the advise of a local realtor, real estate attorney, title company, or other real estate professional."

    (AAI Final Rule, Section IV, R, pg. 66092.)

Note 1: The search by the title search company for environmental cleanup liens also includes institutional controls and other environmental restrictions of record on the title.

Note 2: Title insurance companies are exempted from certain environmental considerations at the property. While that should not stop a title search from identifying a recorded environmental cleanup lien, it appears that in some situations, some title search companies may not include such information on account of the environmental exemption. Because some title companies may deemphasize the need to identify recorded environmental cleanup liens, it is best to clarify this matter with the title search company. Alternately, there are document search and retrieval companies (not affiliated with title companies) that specialize in environmental title searches.

8. **ASTM—Only Recorded Land Title Records:** The revised ASTM Phase I also indicates:
   "Except to the extent that applicable federal, state, local or tribal statutes or regulations specify . . ., environmental liens or activity and use limitations that are recorded or filed any place other than recorded land title records are not considered to be reasonably ascertainable." (ASTM Phase I, E1527-05, Section 6.2.1.)

   "Information about the title to the property that is recorded in a U.S. district court or any place other than where land title records are, by law or custom, recorded for the local jurisdiction in which the property is located, are not considered part of recorded land title records . . . ." (ASTM Phase I, E1527-05, Section 3.2.75. See also Section 8.3.4.4.)

9. **ASTM—Combined Requirements:** Per ASTM, the combined requirements regarding Institutional Controls (IC), Engineering Controls (EC) and recorded environmental cleanup liens are as follows:
   a. IC/EC—Government Records Search (EP): The government records search includes federal and state registries of IC/EC;
   b. IC/EC—Land Title Records (User): The user has an obligation to engage a title company or otherwise provide the EP with (or ask the EP to provide) IC/EC information that may be recorded in land title records;
   c. IC/EC—Other (EP): There are no further mandatory requirements for the EP to search local or other records for IC/EC except for the requirement that *". . . local records and/or additional state or tribal records shall be checked when, in the judgment of the environmental professional, such additional records (1) are reasonable ascertainable, (2) are sufficiently useful, accurate, and complete . . . and (3) are generally obtained, pursuant to local good commercial or customary practice . . . ."* (ASTM Phase I, E1527-05, Section 8.2.2);
   d. Environmental Cleanup Liens (User): The user has an obligation to engage a title company or otherwise provide the EP with (or ask the EP to provide) recorded environmental cleanup liens that are recorded in land title records;
   e. User Questionnaire (EP/User): The User is required to answer the ASTM User Questionnaire in order to assist in gathering material information regarding IC/EC and/or environmental liens. (The User Questionnaire is found at Appendix X3 of the ASTM Phase I.)

[Ref: AAI Final Rule, Subpart C—Standards and Practices, § 312.25 "Searches for Recorded Environmental Cleanup Liens," pg. 66111.]

PART VI: INSPECTION, INTERVIEWS & OTHER REQUIREMENTS

OO. <u>Inspection Requirements for the Subject Property</u>

1. **AAI and ASTM Terminology:**
   - "Inspection," "On-Site Inspection" or "Visual Inspection"—AAI terms.
   - "Site Visit"—ASTM term.
   - "Site Reconnaissance"—ASTM term that describes the information gathering observations performed during a site visit. ASTM uses this term as the title of this portion of a Phase I.

   Note: Informally, U.S. EPA has indicated that it is not intending to impose upon Environmental Professionals a higher standard of care by using the term "inspection" (as opposed to "observation" or "reconnaissance"). (This terminology nuance is of particular concern with many professional liability insurance companies, in that "inspection," as compared to "observation," has historically sometimes been interpreted to denote a heightened degree of professional responsibility.)

2. **U.S. EPA Grantees:** As indicated earlier, for U.S. EPA Grantees, an inspection regarding "hazardous substances" is broadened to hazardous substances, pollutants and contaminants, petroleum and petroleum products and controlled substances.

3. **Who Does the Inspection:** The AAI Final Rule specifically recommends that the inspection be done by an Environmental Professional, although it is not mandated.
   "It continues to be EPA's recommendation that visual inspections of the subject property and adjoining properties be conducted by an individual who meets the regulatory definition of an environmental professional . . . [However] it is not a requirement that the inspection be conducted by an environmental professional. The rule requires only that the inspection be conducted by an individual who is under the supervision or responsible charge of an individual meeting the definition of environmental professional . . . there may be circumstances that in the best professional judgment of an environmental professional, another person under the responsible charge of the environmental professional may be more qualified to conduct the on-site inspection."
   (AAI Final Rule, Section IV, T, pg. 66097.)

4. **Refusal by Seller to Provide Access:** On-site visual inspections are mandatory:
   "In all cases, every effort must be made to conduct an on-site visual inspection of a property when conducting all appropriate inquiries . . . the mere refusal of a property owner to allow the prospective property owner or grantee to have access to the property does not constitute an unusual circumstance, absent the making of good faith efforts to otherwise gain access. The final rule, at § 312.10 defines 'good faith' as 'the absence of any intention to seek an unfair advantage or to defraud another party; an honest and sincere intention to fulfill one's obligation in the conduct or transaction concerned' . . . the final rule requires that the property be visually inspected, or observed, by another method, such as through the use of aerial photography, or be inspected, or observed, from the nearest accessible vantage point, such as the property line or a public road that runs through or along the property."
   (AAI Final Rule, Section IV, T, pg. 66095-96. See also § 312.27, pg. 66112.)

5. **Physical Limitations:** *"Physical limitations to the visual inspection must be noted."*
   (AAI Final Rule, Subpart C—Standards and Practices, § 312.27, Visual Inspections of the Facility and of Adjoining Properties, pg. 66112.)

6. **Other Lack of Access:** In cases of remote or inaccessible locations, or other lack of access, the Environmental Professional must (a) document the efforts undertaken and (b) document other information sources that were consulted and comment on their significance.

> "... documentation should include comments by the environmental professional on the significance of the failure to conduct a visual on-site inspection of the subject property with regard to the ability to identify conditions indicative of releases or threatened releases on, at, in, or to the subject property, if any." (AAI Final Rule, Subpart C—Standard and Practices, § 312.27 Visual Inspection of the Facility and Adjoining Properties (c)(3), pg. 66112.)

> "This documentation should include comments, from the environmental professional who signs the report, regarding any significant limitations on the ability of the environmental professional to identify conditions indicative of releases or threatened releases ... due to the inability of the prospective landowner, grantee, or environmental professional to obtain on-site access to the property." (AAI Final Rule, Section IV, T, pg. 66096.)

7. **ASTM—Who Does the Inspection:** The actual person doing the inspection shall be:

> "a person possessing sufficient training and experience necessary to conduct the site reconnaissance and interviews. . . ."

> "At a minimum, the environmental professional must be involved in planning the site reconnaissance and interviews. Review and interpretation of information upon which the report is based shall be performed by the environmental professional."

(ASTM Phase I, E1527-05, Section 7.5.1.)

8. **ASTM—One Site Visit:** ASTM does not expect more than one site visit in connection with a Phase I Environmental Site Assessment. (ASTM Phase I, E1527-05, Section 9.2.5.)

9. **ASTM—Use of Prior Site Reconnaissance:** Prior reconnaissance information may be used for guidance, but a new site reconnaissance is required. (ASTM Phase I, E1527-05, Section 9.3.)

[Ref: AAI Final Rule, Subpart C—Standards and Practices, § 312.27 "Visual Inspections of the Facility and of Adjoining Properties," pg. 66111-12.]

PP. What Areas and Conditions Must Be Inspected?

1. **What Areas Must Be Inspected:** *". . . [T]he inquiry of the environmental professional must include: (1) a visual on-site inspection of the subject property and facilities and improvements on the subject property, including a visual inspection of the areas where hazardous substances may be or may have been used, stored, treated, handled or disposed."* (AAI Final Rule, Subpart C—Standards and Practices, § 312.27, Visual Inspections of the Facility and of Adjoining Properties, pg. 66111-12.)

2. **ASTM—What Areas Must Be Observed:**
   a. Exterior:
      - The periphery of the property
      - The periphery of all structures
      - The property from all adjacent public thoroughfares
      - Special attention to roads or paths with no apparent outlet
   b. Interior:
      - Accessible common areas
      - Maintenance and repair areas
      - Representative sample of occupant spaces
   c. Miscellaneous:
      - Document the methods or systematic approach (e.g., which spaces were observed, etc.)
      - Document general limitations (e.g., adjacent building obstructions, pavement, water)
      - Document limiting conditions (e.g., rain, snow, etc.)

(ASTM Phase I, E1527-05, Section 9.2.)

3. **ASTM—What Uses and Conditions Must Be Observed:**

Note: ASTM requires that property uses and conditions shall be identified and noted to the extent that they are *"visually and/or physically observed"* on a site visit (or to the extent that they are identified by the interviews or records review).

   a. General Site Setting:
      - Current use(s) of the property
        o Include unoccupied occupant spaces
      - Past use(s) of the property
      - Current uses of adjoining properties
      - Past uses of adjoining properties
      - Current or past uses in the surrounding area
        o "General types of uses"
      - Geologic, hydrogeologic, hydrologic and topographic conditions
        o Include migration potential to or from the property, and into soil or groundwater
      - General description of structures on the property
        o Include stories, age, ancillary structures
      - Roads
        o Adjoining or within property, and parking facilities
      - Potable water supplies
      - Sewage disposal system
        o Include the age of the system

b.   Interior and Exterior Observations:
- Current use(s) of the property
  o Include unoccupied occupant spaces
- Past use(s) of the property
- Hazardous substances and petroleum products
  o Also distinguish if no connection with identified property uses
  o Describe approximate quantities, types of containers and storage conditions
  o Identify past uses that used, treated, stored, disposed of, or generated hazardous substances and/or petroleum products
- Storage tanks (ASTs and USTs)
  o Include vent pipes, fill pies or access ways
  o Include contents, capacity and age;
- Odors
  o Include sources
- Pools of liquids
  o Include sumps, or standing surface water
- Drums (as small as five gallons)
  o Distinguish any leaking drums
- (Other) hazardous substances and/or petroleum products and/or containers
  o Include quantities, container types, storage conditions, etc.
- (Other suspected) unidentified substances containers
- PCBs (i.e., electrical and/or hydraulic equipment)
  o No requirement to note fluorescent light bulbs

c.   Interior Observations
- Heating/Cooling
  o Include fuel sources
- Stains or corrosion
  o Include floors, walls, ceilings, except water stains
- (Floor) drains and sumps

d.   Exterior Observations
- Pits, ponds or lagoons (particularly if associated with waste disposal/treatment)
  o Include if observable on adjoining properties
- Stained soil or pavement
- Stressed vegetation (other than from insufficient water)
- Solid waste
  o Include non-natural fill or unknown fill origin, suspected trash construction or demolition debris, other solid waste disposal, mounds, depressions, etc.
- Waste water
  o Include storm water and any discharge into a drain, ditch, underground injection system or stream on or adjacent to the property
- Wells
  o Include dry wells, irrigation wells, injection wells, abandoned wells, etc.
- Septic systems
  o Include cesspools

(ASTM Phase I, E1527-05, Section 9.4.)

QQ. Inspection Requirements for Adjoining Properties

In addition to inspecting the subject property, the AAI Final Rule requires a visual inspection of adjoining properties.

1. **Definition of Adjoining Properties:** *"Adjoining properties means any real property or properties the border of which is (are) shared in part or in whole with that of the subject property, or that would be shared in part or in whole with that of the subject property but for a street, road, or other public thoroughfare separating the properties."* (AAI Final Rule, Subpart B—Definitions and References, § 312.10 "Definitions and References," pg. 66108.)

2. **Property Line Inspection Acceptable:** The requirement for inspection of adjoining properties is:
    "Visual inspections of adjoining properties may be conducted from the subject property's property line, one or more public rights-of-way, or other vantage point (e.g., via aerial photography). Where practicable, a visual on-site inspection is recommended and may provide greater specificity of information. The visual inspections of adjoining properties must include observing areas where hazardous substances currently may be, or previously may have been, stored, treated, handled, or disposed. Visual inspections of adjoining properties otherwise also must be conducted to achieve the objectives and performance goals for all the appropriate inquiries." (AAI Final Rule, Section IV, T, pg. 66096.)

    Note: Although, where possible, it may theoretically be preferable to have an on-site inspection of adjoining properties, it is commonly recognized that, in most cases, this is not feasible. Firstly, neither a prospective seller nor a prospective landowner may be inclined to reveal their intentions to a neighboring property owner. Secondly, a neighboring property owner may not be inclined to provide access to an inspector working on behalf of a third party.

3. **What Should Be Inspected:** The visual observations of adjoining properties include observing areas where hazardous substances currently may be, or previously may have been, stored, treated, handled or disposed.

    Note: The inspection requirements for adjoining properties are fundamentally no different in nature than for the subject property. The difference lies only in the limitations of conducting the inspections from the property lines, etc.

4. **Physical Limitations:** *"Physical limitations to the visual inspections of adjoining properties should be noted."* (AAI Final Rule, Section IV, T, pg. 66096.)

5. **ASTM—Adjoining Properties:** *"Current Uses of Adjoining Properties—To the extent that current uses of adjoining properties are visually and/or physically observable on the site visit, or are identified in the interviews or records review, they shall be identified in the report and current uses so identified shall be described in the report if they are likely to indicate recognized environmental conditions in connection with the adjoining properties or the property."* (ASTM Phase I, E 1527-05, Section 9.4.1.3.)

[Ref: AAI Final Rule, Subpart C—Standards and Practices, § 312.27 "Visual Inspections of the Facility and of Adjoining Properties" (a)(2), pg. 66111-12.]

61

RR. Interview Requirements

1. **Minimum Interviews:** The current owner and occupant must be interviewed:
   "The final rule requires the environmental professional's inquiry to include interviewing the current owner and occupant of the subject property." (AAI Final Rule, Section IV, P, pg. 66090.)

2. **Additional Interviews:** *"The inquiry of the environmental professional also must include, to the extent necessary to achieve the objectives and performance factors of § 312.20(e) and (f), interviewing one or more of the following persons:*
   [1] Current and past facility managers with relevant knowledge of uses and physical characteristics of the property;
   [2] Past owners, occupants, or operators of the subject property; or
   [3] Employees of current and past occupants of the subject property . . .
   (as necessary to meet the rule's objectives, and in accordance with the performance factors.)"
   (AAI Final Rule, Subpart C—Standards and Practices, § 312.23 "Interviews with Past and Present Owners, Operators and Occupants" (c), pg. 66110; and Section IV, P, pg. 66090.)

   "(W)e assume that the environmental professional will interview only the current property owner if the owner was in the possession of the subject property for more than two years. We assume that after two years of owning a property, the current property owner should have a reasonably good knowledge of its condition." (AAI Final Rule, Section V, 4, pg. 66104.)

3. **Multiple Occupants:** *"In the case of properties where there may be more than one owner or occupant, or many owners or occupants, the final rule requires the inquiry to include interviews of <u>major occupants and those occupants that are using, storing, treating, handling or disposing (or are likely to have used, stored, treated, handled or disposed) of hazardous substances</u> (or pollutants, contaminants, petroleum and petroleum products, and controlled substances, as applicable) on the property. The rule does not specify the number of owners and occupants to be interviewed. The environmental professional must perform this function in the manner that best fulfills the objectives and performance factors for the inquiries in § 312.20(e) and (f). Environmental professionals may use their professional judgment to determine the specific occupants to be interviewed and the total number of occupants to be interviewed . . . Interviews must be conducted with individuals most likely to be knowledgeable about the current and past uses of the property, particularly with regard to current and past uses of hazardous substances on the property."* (AAI Final Rule, Section IV, P, pg. 66090, underlining added; and Subpart C—Standards and Practices, § 312.23 "Interviews with Past and Present, Owners, Operators and Occupants" (b), pg. 66110.)

   Note: If the inspection and interviews are not done by the Environmental Professional, there may be potential complications if the Environmental Professional is not available to select the interviewees.

4. **Neighboring Properties:** Current owners or occupants of neighboring properties may be interviewed as necessary to gather *"commonly known or reasonably ascertainable"* information.

5. **Government Officials:** Under the AAI Final Rule, there is no separate requirement (as is the case with ASTM) to interview local or state government officials, except as may be necessary to gather *"commonly known or reasonably ascertainable"* information.

6. **Abandoned Properties:** *"In the case of inquiries conducted at "abandoned properties," as defined in § 312.10, <u>where there is evidence of potential unauthorized uses of the subject property or evidence of uncontrolled access to the subject property,</u> the environmental professionals must include interviewing one or more (as necessary) owners or occupants of neighboring or nearby properties from which it appears possible to have observed uses of, or releases at, such abandoned properties for the purpose of gathering information necessary to achieve the objectives and performance factors . . . ."* (AAI Final Rule, Subpart C—Standards and Practices, § 312.23 "Interviews with Past and Present Owners, Operators and Occupants" (d), pg. 66110-11, underlining added; and Section IV, P, pg. 66090.)

   Note: An unoccupied property is not necessarily an abandoned property. The AAI Final Rule defines an abandoned property as a *"property that can be presumed to be deserted, or an intent to relinquish possession or control can be inferred from the general disrepair or lack of activity thereon such that a reasonable person could believe that there was an intent on the part of the current owner to surrender rights to the property."* (AAI Final Rule, Subpart B—Definitions, § 312.10, pg. 66108 and Section IV, P, pg. 66090.)

7. **Who Conducts the Interview:** *". . . [A]ll interviews must be conducted by the environmental professional or by someone under the supervision or responsible charge of the environmental professional. The intent is that an individual meeting the definition of an environmental professional (§ 312.10) must oversee the conduct of, or review and approve the results of, the interviews to ensure the interviews are conducted in compliance with the objectives and performance factors (§ 312.20)."* (AAI Final Rule, Section IV, P, pg. 66089-90.)

8. **ASTM—Minimum Interviews:**
   a. Key Site Manager, if possible (e.g., owner, property manager, chief physical plant supervisor or lead maintenance person); plus
   b. A reasonable number of occupants.

9. **ASTM—Additional Interviews:** *"Past Owners, Operators and Occupants—Interviews with past owners, operators and occupants of the property who are likely to have material information regarding the potential for contamination at the property shall be conducted to the extent that they have been identified and that the information likely to be obtained is not duplicative of information already obtained from other sources."* (ASTM Phase I, E1527-05, Section 10.5.4.)

10. **ASTM—Multiple Occupants:**
    a. If there are five or fewer current occupants, attempt to interview all.
    b. If there are six or more current occupants, attempt to interview the major occupant(s) and others whose operations are likely to indicate recognized environmental conditions.
    c. Residential occupants of multifamily properties do not need to be interviewed, except only for any nonresidential occupants.
    d. If above occupants are not available during the site visit, telephone interviews are sufficient.

11. **ASTM—Neighboring Properties:** ASTM has no specific requirement (except for abandoned properties).

12. **ASTM—Government Officials:** A reasonable attempt shall be made to interview at least one staff member of any of the following state and/or local government agencies:
    a. Local fire department;
    b. State and/or local health agency (or local/regional office);
    c. State and/or local hazardous waste or other environmental agency; or
    d. Local building or groundwater use permitting agency.

13. **ASTM—Abandoned Properties:** Similar to AAI language.

14. **ASTM—Who Conducts the Interview:** *"Environmental Professional's Duties—The environmental site assessment must be performed by the environmental professional or conducted under the supervision or responsible charge of the environmental professional. The interviews and site reconnaissance shall be performed by a person possessing sufficient training and experience necessary to conduct the site reconnaissance and interviews in accordance with this practice, and having the ability to identify issues relevant to recognized environmental conditions in connection with the property. At a minimum, the environmental professional must be involved in planning the site reconnaissance and interviews. Review and interpretation of information upon which the report is based shall be performed by the environmental professional."* (ASTM Phase I, E1527-05, Section 7.5.1.)

15. **ASTM—When and How to Interview:** It is within the discretion of the EP when and how to ask questions. It can be before, during or after the site visit. It can be in person, by telephone or in writing.

SS. Interview Questions

1. **Interview Questions:** *"The AAI Final Rule does not prescribe particular questions that must be asked during the interview. The type and content of any questions asked during interviews will depend upon the site-specific conditions and circumstances and the extent of the environmental professional's (or other individual's under the supervision or responsible charge of the environmental professional) knowledge of the property prior to conducting the interviews."* (AAI Final Rule, Section IV, P, pg. 66090.)

2. **ASTM—Interview Questions:** Questions should focus on:

   a. uses and conditions observed during the site reconnaissance;

   b. helpful documents including:
      - Environmental site assessment reports
      - Environmental compliance audit reports
      - Environmental permits (for example, solid waste disposal permits, hazardous waste disposal permits, wastewater permits, NPDES permits, underground injection permits)
      - Registrations for underground and above-ground storage tanks
      - Registrations for underground injection systems
      - Material safety data sheets
      - Community right-to-know plan
      - Safety plans; preparedness and prevention plans; spill prevention, countermeasure and control plans; etc.
      - Reports regarding hydrogeologic conditions on the property or surrounding area
      - Notices or other correspondence from any government agency relating to past or current violations of environmental laws with respect to the property or relating to environmental liens encumbering the property
      - Hazardous waste generator notices or reports
      - Geotechnical studies
      - Risk assessments
      - Recorded AULs

      (ASTM Phase I, E1527-05, Section 10.8.1.)

c. proceedings involving the property, including:

"*(1) any pending, threatened, or past litigation relevant to hazardous substances or petroleum products in, on, or from the property;*

(2) any pending, threatened, or past administrative proceedings relevant to hazardous substances or petroleum products in, on, or from the property; and

(3) any notices from any governmental entity regarding any possible violation of environmental laws or possible liability relating to hazardous substances or petroleum products."

(ASTM Phase I, E1527-05, Section 10.9.)

d. Uses and conditions regarding:
- Pits, Ponds or Lagoons
- Stained Soil or Pavement
- Stressed Vegetation
- Solid Waste
- Waste Water
- Wells
- Septic Systems

(See ASTM Phase I, E1527-05, Section 9.4.4.)

Note: The last set of questions (i.e., pits, ponds . . . septic systems) are intended to duplicate the same items to be observed during the site reconnaissance exterior observations.

Note 1: ASTM acknowledges that interviewees (except for the user or the user's key site manager) do not necessarily have an obligation to answer questions.

Note 2: ASTM requires that unanswered or incomplete answers be documented in writing or, if the questions were asked in writing, that at least one reasonable follow-up telephone call or written request is made.

Note 3: ASTM requires that the questions regarding helpful documents (ASTM Phase I, E1527-05, Section 10.8.1) and proceedings involving the property (ASTM Phase I, E1527-05, Section 10.9) be asked prior to the site visit.

TT. Specialized Knowledge of the Prospective Landowner

1. Specialized knowledge or experience on the part of the person undertaking the inquiry (prospective landowner or grantee): *"(a) persons to whom this part is applicable per § 312.1(b) must take into account their specialized knowledge of the subject property, the area surrounding the subject property, the conditions of adjoining properties, and any other experience relevant to the inquiry, for the purpose of identifying conditions indicative of releases or threatened releases* (of hazardous substances) *at the subject property . . . ."*

2. *(b) All appropriate inquiries, as outlined in § 312.20, are not complete unless the results of the inquiries take into account the relevant and applicable specialized knowledge and experience of the persons responsible for undertaking the inquiry (as described in § 312.1(b))."*

3. This does not include any requirement beyond what has been previously required under CERCLA. *"Nothing in (the) rule changes the nature or intent of this requirement as it has existed in the statute since 1986."* (AAI Final Rule, Section IV, U, pg. 66097.)

Note 1: This item is the responsibility of the prospective landowner (or Grantee) and not the Environmental Professional.

Note 2: The specialized knowledge of the prospective landowner (or Grantee) may include that of persons working for the prospective landowner (or Grantee).

Note 3: The components of an AAI which are the responsibility of the prospective landowner (or Grantee) should be provided to the Environmental Professional. However, there is no mandate that these items must be shared with the EP. In situations where the information is not shared, however, the Environmental Professional must address the impact of such lack of information on his/her ability to make an opinion. If there is an impact, then the Environmental Professional must treat it as a data gap. (See AAI Final Rule, Section III, pg. 66076.)

4. **ASTM:** *"Specialized Knowledge or Experience of the User—If the user is aware of any specialized knowledge or experience that is material to recognized environmental conditions in connection with the property, it is the user's responsibility to communicate any information based on such specialized knowledge or experience to the environmental professional. The user should do so before the environmental professional conducts the site reconnaissance."* (ASTM Phase I, E1527-05, Section 6.3.)

5. **ASTM:** *"Actual Knowledge of the User—If the user has actual knowledge of any environmental liens or AULs encumbering the property or in connection with the property, it is the user's responsibility to communicate such information to the environmental professional. The user should do so before the environmental professional conducts the site reconnaissance."* (ASTM Phase I, E1527-05, Section 6.4.)

6. **ASTM:** ASTM provides a "User Questionnaire" which the User must answer. It is designed to address the above four requirements of the prospective landowner (as well as information regarding Activity and Use Limitations and Environmental Liens). The User Questionnaire is found at Appendix X3 of the ASTM Phase I.

[Ref: AAI Final Rule, Subpart C—Standards and Practices, § 312.28 "Specialized Knowledge or Experience on the Part of the Defendant," pg. 66112.]

UU. Relationship of Purchase Price to Value

Include the relationship of the purchase price to the (fair market) value of the property if the property was not contaminated.

1. The AAI Final Rule requires that the purchaser of the property *"must consider whether or not the purchase price of the subject property reasonably reflects the fair market value of the property if the property were not contaminated."*

2. The AAI Final Rule requires that the purchaser consider whether any differential between the purchase price and the noncontaminated fair market value of the property is due to the presence of releases or threatened releases of hazardous substances.

3. The AAI Final Rule does not require that a formal real estate appraisal be conducted for the purchaser to make a general determination of whether the price paid for a property reflects its market value. Such a determination may be made by comparing the price paid for a particular property to prices paid for similar properties located in the same vicinity as the subject property, or by consulting a real estate expert familiar with properties in the general locality and who may be able to provide a comparability analysis.

4. The objective is not to ascertain the exact value of the property, but to determine whether or not the purchase price paid for the property is reflective of its market value. Significant differences in the purchase price and market value of a property should be noted and the reasons for any differences should be noted.

5. **ASTM:** *"Reason for Significantly Lower Purchase Price—. . . the user shall consider the relationship of the purchase price of the property to the fair market value of the property if the property was not affected by hazardous substances or petroleum products. The user should try to identify an explanation for a lower price which does not reasonably reflect fair market value if the property were not contaminated, and make a written record of such explanation. Among the factors to consider will be the information that becomes known to the user pursuant to the Phase I Environmental Site Assessment. This standard does not require that a real estate appraisal be obtained in order to ascertain fair market value of the property."* (ASTM Phase I, E1527-05, Section 6.5.)

    Note: This item is the responsibility of the prospective landowner (or Grantee) and not the Environmental Professional.

[Ref: AAI Final Rule, Subpart C—Standards and Practices, § 312.29 "The Relationship of the Purchase Price to the Value of the Property, if the Property was Not Contaminated," pg. 66112.]

VV. Commonly Known or Reasonably Ascertainable Information

Include commonly known or reasonably ascertainable information about the property.

1. *"Commonly known or reasonably ascertainable information includes information about a property that generally is known to the public within the community where the property is located and can be easily sought and found from individuals familiar with the property or from easily attainable public sources of information . . . (The) rule does not change the nature or intent of this requirement as it has existed in the statute since 1986."*
    (AAI Final Rule, Section IV, W, pg. 66099-100.)

2. Commonly known or reasonably ascertainable information generally is information available in the local community that may be ascertained from the owner or occupant of a property, owners or occupants of neighboring properties to the subject property, local or state government officials, local media sources, community organizations, local libraries, historical societies and members of the local community.
    "For example, neighboring property owners and local community members may have information regarding undocumented uses of a property during periods when the property was idle or abandoned."
    (AAI Final Rule, Section IV, W, pg. 66100.)

3. *"To the extent necessary to achieve the objectives and performance factors of § 312.20(e) and (f), persons to whom this part is applicable per § 312.1(b) [perspective purchaser or grantee] and the environmental professional must gather information from varied sources whose input either individually or taken together may provide commonly known or reasonably ascertainable information about the subject property;*
    The environmental professional may refer to <u>one or more</u> of the following sources of information:
    (1) current owners or occupants of neighboring properties or properties adjacent to the subject property;
    (2) local and state government officials who may have knowledge of, or information related to, the subject property; (3) others with knowledge of the subject property; and (4) other sources of information (e.g., newspapers, websites, community organizations, local libraries and historical societies."
    (AAI Final Rule, Subpart C—Standards and Practices, § 312.30 "Commonly Known or Reasonable Ascertainable Information about the Property" (c), pg. 66112, underlining added.)

4. *"<u>This information may be incidental to other information collected</u> during the inquiries, and separate or distinct efforts to collect the information may not be necessary . . . The collection and use of commonly known information about a property may be done in connection with the collection of all other required information for the purposes of achieving the objectives and performance factors contained in § 312.20 . . . The requirement is not meant to require exhaustive data collection efforts . . . The intent of the requirement is to establish that a prospective landowner or grantee and an environmental professional conducting all appropriate inquiries on his or her behalf must make efforts to collect and consider information about a property that is commonly known within the local community or that can be reasonable ascertained."* (AAI Final Rule, Section IV, W, pg. 66100, underlining added.)

    Note: This requirement applies to both the Environmental Professional and the prospective landowner (or Grantee). *"Throughout the inquiries, persons to whom this part is applicable per § 312.1(b) [prospective landowners and Grantees] and environmental professionals conducting the inquiry must take into account. . . ."* (AAI Final Rule, Subpart C—Standards and Practices, § 312.30 "Commonly Known or Reasonable Ascertainable Information about the Property" (a), pg. 66112.)

5. **ASTM:** *"Commonly Known or Reasonably Ascertainable Information—If the user is aware of any commonly known or reasonably ascertainable information within the local community about the property that is material to recognized environmental conditions in connection with the property, it is the user's responsibility to communicate such information to the environmental professional. The user should do so before the environmental professional conducts the site reconnaissance."* (ASTM Phase I, E1527-05, Section 6.6.)

WW. Degree of Obviousness

Include the degree of obviousness of the presence or likely presence of contamination at the property, and the ability to detect the contamination by appropriate investigation.

1. **Take into Account All Information:** *"(a) Persons to whom this part is applicable per § 312.1(b) and environmental professionals conducting an inquiry of a property on behalf of such persons must take into account the information collected under § 312.23 through 312.30 in considering the degree of obviousness of the presence of releases or threatened releases at the subject property (and)*
   (b) . . . in considering the ability to detect contamination by appropriate investigation."
   (AAI Final Rule, Subpart C—Standards and Practices, § 312.31 "The Degree of Obviousness of the Presence or Likely Presence of Contamination at the Property, and the Ability to Detect the Contamination by Appropriate Investigation," pg. 66112-13.)

2. **Consider All Information in Total:** *"The final rule requires that persons conducting all appropriate inquiries consider all the information collected during the conduct of the inquiries in totality to ascertain the potential presence of a release or threatened release at the property. Persons conducting all appropriate inquiries, following the collection of all required information, must assess whether or not an obvious conclusion may be drawn that there are conditions indicative of a release or threatened release of hazardous substances . . . all the information should be considered in total to determine whether or not there are indications of releases or threatened releases."* (AAI Final Rule, Section IV, X, pg. 66101.)

3. **No Requirement to Collect Additional Information:** *"We [U.S. EPA] interpret the statutory criterion to require consideration of information already obtained during the conduct of all appropriate inquiries investigation and not as a requirement to collect additional information."* (AAI Final Rule, Section IV, X, pg. 66101.)

4. **No Change to CERCLA:** *"Nothing in the AAI Final Rule is intended to change the nature or intent of this requirement as it has existed in the statute since 1986."* (AAI Final Rule, Section IV, X, pg. 66101.)

5. **Opinion Regarding Additional Appropriate Investigations:** *"The inquiry of the environmental professional should include an opinion regarding additional appropriate investigations, if any."* (AAI Final Rule, Subpart C—Standards and Practices, § 312.31 "The Degree of Obviousness of the Presence or Likely Presence of Contamination at the Property, and the Ability to Detect the Contamination by Appropriate Investigation," pg. 66113.)

   (See also Part CCC: Additional Appropriate Investigations.)

6. **ASTM—Degree of Obviousness:** ASTM includes this requirement within the overall Phase I Environmental Site Assessment.

Note: This requirement applies principally to the Environmental Professional. However, the prospective landowner (or Grantee) also shares in this requirement. (See § 312.31, pg. 66112.)

PART VII: REPORT PREPARATION REQUIREMENTS

XX. Report Format

1. **Written Documentation:** The Environmental Professional must document the "All Appropriate Inquiry" in a written report.

2. **No Required Format:** There is no prescriptive format.

   The Environmental Professional may design and develop the format and content to meet the prospective landowner's objectives and information needs in addition to providing documentation that "All Appropriate Inquiries" were completed.

   "The provisions of the final rule allow for the property owner (or grantee) and any environmental professional engaged in the conduct of all appropriate inquiries for a specific property to design and develop the format and content of a written report that will meet the prospective landowner's (or grantee's) objectives and information needs in addition to providing documentation that all appropriate inquiries were completed prior to the acquisition of the property." (AAI Final Rule, Section IV, D, pg. 66078.)

4. **ASTM—Written Documentation:** ASTM requires that findings, opinions and conclusions be documented or referenced, and which includes documentation of sources that revealed no findings. (ASTM Phase I, E1527-05, Sections 12.2 and 12.5.)

5. **ASTM—Recommended Format:** ASTM has a recommended report format (which is found in Appendix X4 of the ASTM Phase I).

6. **ASTM—Identify Personnel:** ASTM requires identification of the Environmental Professional and the person who conducted the site reconnaissance and interviews. (ASTM Phase I, E1527-05, Section 12.3.)

7. **ASTM—Document Whether the User Provided Information:** ASTM requires that the report state whether the user provided information regarding:
   a. Title and judicial records for Environmental Liens or Activity and Use Limitations (AULs),
   b. Specialized knowledge or experience of the user,
   c. Actual knowledge of the user,
   d. Reason for significantly lower purchaser price, and
   e. Commonly known or reasonably ascertainable information.
   (ASTM Phase I, E1527-05, Section 12.3.)

YY. Professional Opinion

1. **Opinions:** The Environmental Professional must:
   a. provide an opinion as to whether the "All Appropriate Inquiry" identified conditions indicative of releases or threatened releases of hazardous substances on, at, in or to the subject property;
   b. identify any data gaps in the information developed that affect the ability to identify conditions indicative of releases or threatened releases of hazardous substances;
   c. comment regarding the significance of the data gaps with regard to the ability to identify conditions indicative of releases or threatened releases of hazardous substances;
   d. comment regarding the significance of the data gaps on the Environmental Professional's ability to provide an opinion as to whether the "All Appropriate Inquiries" have identified conditions indicative of releases or threatened releases;
   e. identify the sources of information consulted to address, or fill, such data gaps;
   f. provide an opinion regarding additional appropriate investigation, if any may be necessary.
   (Note: See CCC: Additional Appropriate Investigations.)

2. **U.S. EPA Grantees:** Opinions for U.S. EPA Grantees must also encompass pollutants and contaminants, petroleum and petroleum products and controlled substances.

3. **ASTM—Opinions:** The Environmental Professional:
   a. Shall provide an opinion which shall include the logic, reasoning and rationale relating to the investigation and for concluding whether a condition is or is not currently a recognized environmental condition.
   b. Should provide an opinion regarding additional appropriate investigation (See CCC: Additional Appropriate Investigations).
   c. *"Shall identify and comment on significant data gaps that affect the ability of the environmental professional to identify recognized environmental conditions."*
   d. Shall *". . . identify the sources of information that were consulted to address the data gaps."*
   (ASTM Phase I, E1527-05, Sections 12.6 and 12.7.)

[Ref: AAI Final Rule, Subpart C—Standards and Practices, § 312.21 "Results of Inquiry by an Environmental Professional," pg. 66110; and Section IV, D, pg. 66077-78.]

ZZ. Conformance Declarations

1. **Declarations:** The report must state that the individual completing the work met the definition of an Environmental Professional, and that the Phase I inquiry was completed in accordance with the federal "All Appropriate Inquiries" Rule.

    The required declarations (above the signature) are as follows:

    "[I, We] declare that, to the best of [my, our] professional knowledge and belief, [I, we] meet the definition of Environmental Professional as defined in § 312.21 of 40 CFR part 312."

    "[I, We] have the specific qualifications based on education, training, and experience to assess a property of the nature, history and setting of the subject property."

    "[I, We] developed and performed the all appropriate inquiries in conformance with the standards and practices set forth in 40 CFR part 312."

2. **Signature:** The report must be signed by the Environmental Professional.

3. **Qualifications:** The qualifications of the Environmental Professional must be included.

4. **No Certifications or Seals Required:** Environmental Professionals do not have to "certify" the results of the AAI when signing the report. P.E.s and P.G.s also do not have to include a professional seal. (AAI Final Rule, Section IV, D, pg. 66077.)

5. **ASTM—Conclusions/Declarations:** The Phase I shall include a conclusions section that summarizes all recognized environmental conditions, and which includes one of the following statements:

    > *"We have performed a Phase I Environmental Site Assessment*
    > *in conformance with the scope and limitations of ASTM Practice E1527*
    > *of [insert address or legal description], the property.*
    > *Any exceptions to, or deletions from, this practice*
    > *are described in Section [ ] of this report.*
    > *This assessment has revealed no evidence*
    > *of recognized environmental conditions in connection with the property."*
    > > -or-
    > *"We have performed a Phase I Environmental Site Assessment*
    > *in conformance with the scope and limitations of ASTM Practice E1527*
    > *of [insert address or legal description], the property.*
    > *Any exceptions to, or deletions from, this practice*
    > *are described in Section [ ] of this report.*
    > *This assessment has revealed no evidence*
    > *of recognized environmental conditions in connection with the property*
    > *except for the following: (list)."*

    (ASTM Phase I, E1527-05, Section 12.8.1 and 12.8.2.)

    In addition, the AAI requires that the AAI conformance declarations shall be included.

6. **ASTM—Signature:** The Environmental Professional shall sign the report. (ASTM Phase I, E1527-05, Section 12.12.)

7. **ASTM—Appendix and Qualifications:** An appendix shall be included, containing supporting documentation and the qualifications of the Environmental Professional and personnel who conducted the site reconnaissance and interviews. (ASTM Phase I, E1527-05, Section 12.14.)

8. **ASTM—Other Requirements:**
   a. Additional services should only be included if so specified in the terms of engagement.
   b. All deletions, deviations and additions shall be listed.
   c. References shall be included.

   (ASTM Phase I, E1527-05, Sections 12.9, 12.10, 12.11.)

[Ref: AAI Final Rule, Subpart C—Standards and Practices, § 312.21 "Results of Inquiry by an Environmental Professional," pg. 66110.]

AAA. Time Constraints (Shelf Life)

1. **Prior to Acquisition:** The All Appropriate Inquiries must be completed by the date of acquisition of the property. No part of an AAI/Phase I may be done subsequent to property acquisition.
    > *"Prospective landowners who do not conduct all appropriate inquiries prior to or on the date of obtaining ownership of the property may lose their ability to claim protection from CERLCA liability as an innocent landowner, bona fide prospective purchaser, or contiguous property owner . . . . Any party seeking liability protection . . . must conduct all appropriate inquiries prior to or on the date of acquiring a property.*
    (AAI Final Rule, Section I, A, pg. 66070.)

    > *"Date of acquisition or purchase date means the date on which a person acquires title to the property."*
    (AAI Final Rule, Subpart B—Definitions, § 312.10, pg. 66108.)

2. **Six-Month/Twelve-Month Shelf Life:** The following items must be completed no more than six (6) months prior to property acquisition: (a) interviews with past and present owners, operators and occupants; (b) searches for recorded environmental cleanup liens; (c) reviews of federal, tribal, state and local government records; (d) visual inspections of the facility and of adjoining properties; and (e) the Environmental Professional conformance declarations.

    The balance of the Phase I must be completed within one year prior to property acquisition. Phase Is older than one year have to be updated. Time is counted not from the date of the report, but the date when the work was done.

3. **Using Previously Collected Information:** With regard to using previously collected information:
    > *". . . in all cases where a prospective landowner is using previously collected information, the all appropriate inquiries for the current purchase must be updated to include a summary of any relevant changes to the conditions of the property and any specialized knowledge of the prospective landowner."*
    (AAI Final Rule, Section IV, J, pg. 66084.)

4. **Using Information from Previous Assessments:**
    > *"In (the) final rule, we . . . allow for the use of information contained in previously-conducted assessments, even if the information was collected more than a year prior to the date on which the subject property is acquired. The final rule does require that all aspects of a site assessment, or all appropriate inquiries investigation, completed more than one year prior to the date of acquisition of the subject property be updated to reflect current conditions and current property-specific information."* (AAI Final Rule, Section III, pg. 66075.)

    > *". . . [I]f the prior all appropriate inquiries investigation was completed more than a year prior to the property acquisition date, all parts of the investigation must be reviewed and updated for the all appropriate inquiries to be complete."* (AAI Final Rule, Section IV, I, pg. 66083.)

5. **ASTM—Six-Month/Twelve-Month Shelf Life:** ASTM Phase I requirements are similar to the above AAI requirements. (See ASTM Phase I, E1527-05, Section 4.6.)

6. **ASTM—Using Previously Collected Information/Assessments:** *". . . [S]uch information shall not be used without current investigation of conditions likely to affect recognized environmental conditions. . . ."* (ASTM Phase I, E1527-05, Section 4.7.1.)

[Ref: AAI Final Rule, Subpart C—Standards and Practices, § 312.20 "All Appropriate Inquiries" (b)(c), pg. 66109.]

BBB. <u>No Government Reporting Requirement</u>

1. There are no new government reporting requirements. There is no requirement to notify U.S. EPA or any other government entity.

    "(d) Disclosure obligations. None of the requirements of this part limit or expand disclosure obligation under any federal, state, tribal, or local law. . . ." (AAI Final Rule, Subpart A—Introduction, § 312.1, pg. 66108.)

    "The final rule does not include any new reporting or disclosure obligations . . . [The] rule contains no new requirements to notify or submit information to EPA or any other government entity."
    (AAI Final Rule, Section IV, C, pg. 66077.)

2. However, all current reporting requirements remain in effect.
    "Although today's rule does not include any new disclosure requirements, CERCLA section 103 does require persons in charge of vessels and facilities, including on-shore and off-shore facilities, to notify the National Response Center of any release of a hazardous substance from the vessel or facility in a quantity equal to or greater than a 'reportable quantity,' as defined in CERCLA section 102(b). Today's rule includes no changes to this reporting requirement nor any changes to any other reporting or disclosure requirements under federal, tribal, or state law."
    (Final Rule, Section IV C, Federal Register pg. 66077, www.epa.gov/swerosps/bf/aai/aai_final_rule.pdf.)

PART VIII: ADDITIONAL INVESTIGATIONS & PHASE IIS

CCC. Additional Appropriate Investigations

1. **What Are "Additional Investigations":** Both the AAI Final Rule and the ASTM Phase I are silent as to what exactly constitutes "Additional Investigations." They conceivably may include:
    a. "more of the same," i.e., more records searches, historical searches, site inspection, interviews, etc; or
    b. Phase II sampling and analysis.

2. **Requirement Regarding "Additional Appropriate Investigation":** The AAI Final Rule includes "Additional Appropriate Investigation" as part of the AAI requirement to include *the degree of obviousness of the presence or likely presence of contamination at the property and the ability to detect the contamination by appropriate investigation."*

    "Persons . . . and environmental professionals conducting an inquiry of a property on behalf of such persons must take into account the information collected under § 312.23 through § 312.30 <u>in considering the ability to detect contamination</u> by appropriate investigation. The inquiry of the environmental professional should <u>include an opinion regarding additional appropriate investigation, if any.</u>" (AAI Final Rule, Subpart C— Standards and Practices, § 312.31 "The Degree of Obviousness of the Presence or Likely Presence of Contamination at the Property, and the Ability to Detect the Contamination by Appropriate Investigation," pg. 66113, underlining added.)

Note 1: § 312.23 through § 312.30 refers to all the components of an "All Appropriate Inquiries" that are the responsibility of the Environmental Professional, but not the four "Additional Inquiries" that are the responsibility of the user. (See also Part CC: Components of the "All Appropriate Inquiries" Assessment.)

> *"The final rule also retains the proposed requirement that the environmental professional include as part of the results of his or her inquiry an opinion regarding additional appropriate investigation, if any may be necessary . . . <u>the environmental professional should provide an opinion regarding whether or not additional investigation is necessary to detect potential contamination at the site, if in his or her opinion there are conditions indicative of releases or threatened releases of hazardous substances</u> . . . Nothing in (the) rule changes the nature of intent of this requirement as it has existed in the statute since 1986."*
> (AAI Final Rule, Section IV, X, pg. 66101, underlining added.)

Note 2: The AAI language suggests that additional appropriate investigations may include the need to recommend Phase II sampling and analysis when the additional appropriate investigation has identified "conditions indicative of releases." (If so, such opinions, nonetheless, remain within the professional judgment of the Environmental Professional.)

3. **ASTM—Requirement Regarding "Additional Appropriate Investigation"**: ASTM is similarly not specific as to what exactly constitutes "Additional Investigation."

> "*Additional Investigation—The environmental professional should provide an opinion regarding additional appropriate investigation, if any, to detect the presence of hazardous substances or petroleum products. This opinion should only be provided in the unusual circumstance when greater certainty is required regarding the identified recognized environmental conditions. A Phase I Environmental Site Assessment which includes such an opinion by the environmental professional does not render the assessment incomplete. <u>This opinion is not intended to constitute a requirement that the environmental professional include any recommendations for Phase II</u> or other assessment activities.*" (ASTM Phase I, E1527-05, Section 12.6.1, underlining added.)

Note 1: The ASTM language is more directed at using additional appropriate investigations to "firm up" whether a concern is or is not a REC, i.e., it is an opinion directed at the obviousness of a REC (and not whether an already identified REC should be further investigated with Phase II sampling and analysis).

ASTM has a separate requirement that a recommendation for Phase II testing not be made unless the user agrees for a recommendation to be made. Thus, the language here regarding "Additional Investigation" also clarifies that the separate Phase II recommendation restriction is not altered or overridden.

Note 2: It is the general intent, within the ASTM Phase I, for the Environmental Professional to have to decide whether a situation does or does not constitute a Recognized Environmental Condition (REC). Opinions regarding additional investigations should preferably not be made in order to avoid determining whether a situation is or is not a REC. However, it is recognized that some RECs may simply require, per the judgment of the Environmental Professional, more investigation in order for the Environmental Professional to be able to characterize the REC with sufficient certainty.

Note 3: There could also be situations where the Environmental Professional may need to address the need for additional investigations for issues that are not necessarily identified as "Recognized Environmental Conditions" (RECs). The ASTM language (which specifically addresses RECs) is not intended to inhibit the Environmental Professional from addressing those situations which are not identified as RECs.

DDD. Phase II Sampling & Analysis

1. **Sampling and Analysis May Sometimes Need to Be Done:** There is no requirement per se within the AAI Final Rule to conduct Phase II sampling and analysis in order to receive AAI liability protections. Recommendations regarding Phase II sampling and analysis are an option for Environmental Professionals depending on the particular circumstances.

> *"With regard to the conduct of sampling and analysis, (the) final rule does not require sampling and analysis as part of the all appropriate inquiries investigation."* (AAI Final Rule, Section IV, X, pg. 66101.)

> *"However, sampling and analysis may be valuable in determining the possible presence and extent of potential contamination at a property. In addition, the fact that the all appropriate inquiry standards do not require sampling and analysis does not prevent a court from concluding that, under the circumstances of a particular case, sampling and analysis should have been conducted to meet "the degree of obviousness of the presence or likely presence of contamination at the property, and the ability to detect the contamination by appropriate investigation" criterion and obtain protection from CERCLA liability . . . In certain instances, depending upon site-specific circumstances and the totality of the information collected during the all appropriate inquiries prior to the property acquisition, it may be necessary to conduct sampling and analysis either pre- or post-acquisition, to fully understand the conditions at a property, and fully comply with the statutory requirements for the CERCLA liability protections. In addition, sampling and analysis may help explain existing data gaps."* (AAI Final Rule, Section IV, X, pg. 66101.)

Note: The question whether to obtain a Phase II would be especially relevant where it appears that the property has been contaminated and where the prospective landowner does want to receive the Bona Fide Prospective Purchaser liability protection.

2. **ASTM—No Testing or Sampling in a Phase I:** The revised ASTM Phase I does not include any testing or sampling except only with the contractual agreement of the user (ASTM Phase I, E1527-05, Section 7.4).

> *"Additional Services—Any additional services contracted for between the user and the environmental professional(s), including a broader scope of assessment, more detailed conclusions, liability/risk evaluations, <u>recommendation for Phase II testing</u>, remediation techniques, etc., are beyond the scope of this practice, and <u>should only be included in the report if so specified in the terms of engagement between the user and the environmental professional.</u>"* (ASTM Phase I, E1527-05, Section 12.9, underlining added.)

Note: Notwithstanding the above, if the user has indicated to the Environmental Professional that the user wishes the Phase I to be done per AAI, then there may be an implicit approval for the Environmental Professional to issue a recommendation regarding Phase II sampling and analysis without further authorization by the user.

3. **How Much Phase II Sampling and Analysis Is Enough:** Phase II sampling and analysis has been historically understood to mean an iterative process to, first, confirm the suspicions of the Phase I, and, then, to quantify and characterize the contamination, leading toward the enabling of remediation to be conducted.

> *"6.1 Objective and Purpose—The objective of conducting a Phase II ESA [Environmental Site Assessment] is to evaluate the recognized environmental conditions identified in the Phase I ESA or transaction screen process. The purpose of conducting a Phase II ESA depends on the objective(s) of the user. Typically, the purposes of a Phase II ESA are to:*
>
> *6.1.1 Develop sufficient information from which the environmental professional reasonably can render a professional opinion that, with respect to the recognized environmental conditions assessed, hazardous substances have not been disposed or released at the property, thereby satisfying the innocent purchaser defense under CERCLA as to those recognized environmental conditions; or*
>
> *6.1.2 Develop sufficient information about the presence of a recognized environmental condition at a site to meet the business objectives of the user and to provide sufficient data to assist the user in making informed business decisions, or both.*
>
> *6.1.3 The Phase II work scope may consist of several iterations and may be terminated at any point, once the objectives of the user have been satisfied."*

(Standard Guide for Environmental Site Assessments: Phase II Environmental Site Assessment Process, ASTM E1903-97 (Reapproved 2002).)

Per the AAI Final Rule, it may not be necessary to fully quantify and characterize contamination to support a cost estimate for the overall cleanup of a property, in order to receive and maintain the CERCLA landowner liability protections, because (complete) remediation may no longer be the goal. Continuing Obligations are not intended to obligate protected landowners to traditional CERCLA cleanups. If a protected landowner does not have to cleanup, then the protected landowner may—perhaps—need only to quantify and characterize as needed to (a) document that all contamination occurred prior to acquisition, and to (b) fully understand the conditions of the property for "continuing obligation" purposes (but not for "cleanup" purposes).

Limited Phase II sampling and analysis investigations "to confirm the presence" of contaminants are already countenanced by the current ASTM standard guide.

> *"1.3.1 The mere confirmation of contamination or the preliminary indication of the extent and magnitude of contamination may be sufficient for the purposes of many users. If a user desires a more complete characterization of the environmental condition of the property, further assessment may be undertaken."*

> *"8.1 The assessment activities to be conducted under the Phase II ESA may range from field screening methods to intrusive multi-media sampling and laboratory analysis."*

(Standard Guide for Environmental Site Assessments: Phase II Environmental Site Assessment Process, ASTM E1903-97 (Reapproved 2002).)

Note: The ASTM Phase II (E1903) is currently being re-evaluated per the above considerations.

4. **What Are the Goals of the Prospective Landowner?**
    a. A Phase II sampling and analysis investigation is not an "off the shelf" item to be conducted. A Phase II needs to reflect the requirements, circumstances and goals of the (new) landowner.
    b. For example, a prospective landowner intending on using the property for warehousing of benign consumer goods may not need the same Phase II documentation as would be the case if an industrial facility was being planned for the property. (However, if a voluntary cleanup was being planned, or a school was intended on being built, much more intensive sampling and analysis would likely be needed.)
    c. It is conceivable that on the one hand, in order to document that all contamination occurred prior to acquisition, there may be an increase in Phase II Sampling and Analysis in the marketplace; and on the other hand, such Phase IIs may be more customized to the needs of the prospective landowner.

EEE. When Should Additional Appropriate Investigations and Phase IIs Be Done?

1. The AAI Final Rule is <u>silent as to whether additional investigations</u> should be done pre- or post-acquisition. The AAI Final Rule <u>explicitly permits Phase II sampling and analysis</u> both before and after acquisition. (See also AAI Final Rule, Subpart C—Standards and Practices, § 312.31 "The Degree of Obviousness of the Presence or Likely Presence of Contamination at the Property, and the Ability to Detect the Contamination by Appropriate Investigation," pg. 66113.)

   "In certain instances, depending on site-specific circumstances and the totality of the information collected during the all appropriate inquiries prior to the property acquisition, it may be necessary to conduct sampling and analysis either pre or post-acquisition to fully understand the conditions at a property, and fully comply with the statutory requirements for the CERCLA liability protections. In addition, sampling and analysis may help explain existing data gaps. Prospective landowners should be mindful of all the statutory requirements for obtaining the CERCLA liability protections when considering whether or not to conduct sampling and analysis prior to or after acquiring a property. (The) final regulation does not require that sampling and analysis be conducted as part of the all appropriate inquiries investigation."
   (AAI Final Rule, Section IV, X, pg. 66101-102.)

2. The ASTM Phase I is <u>silent as to whether additional investigations</u> should be done pre- or post-acquisition. (See ASTM Phase I, E1527-05, Section 12.6.1.) The ASTM Phase I does not include Phase II sampling and analysis within the Phase I except when the user contracts for such (ASTM Phase I, E1527-05, Section 7.4). Assuming user willingness, the ASTM Phase I <u>would permit Phase II sampling and analysis</u> both before and after acquisition.

3. At the same time, the ASTM Phase I permits the scope of the Phase I to include "remediation techniques, etc.," within a Phase I (subject to concurrence between the Environmental Professional and user). In addition, there is nothing to prevent an Environmental Professional and user from conducting sampling and analysis (or reviewing a previously conducted sampling and analysis investigation) and then including the results, and accompanying opinions, including "remediation techniques" or other "more detailed conclusions," within an AAI/ASTM Phase I report.

FFF. Vapor Intrusion

1. **Definition of Vapor Intrusion:** Vapor intrusion means the release or migration of volatile chemicals from contaminated soil, groundwater or other sources. For example, gas stations, dry cleaners or other industrial facilities may be the source of CERCLA hazardous substances (e.g., benzene, trichloroethylene, perchloroethylene, etc.). These volatile chemicals can enter the airspace of nearby structures and thereby contaminate those structures.

2. **Not Yet Common Practice in Phase I & IIs:** Vapor intrusion testing and analysis is a relatively new phenomenon, and has not yet received widespread consideration. Although, to date, vapor intrusion has not been a common focus of Phase Is and IIs (i.e., most testing continues to be for soil, surface water, groundwater, sediments, bedrock and other materials, e.g., PCBs, etc.), vapor intrusion is increasingly becoming an additional focus of hazardous substances investigations.

3. **ASTM—Indirectly Addressed:** The ASTM Phase I does not address vapor intrusion directly. However, it does make provision for addressing vapor intrusion in that a Recognized Environmental Condition includes a release *"into structures on the property."* (ASTM Phase I, E1527-05, Section 1.1.1.)

4. **For More Information:**
    a. Federal—More information can be obtained from "(Draft) Guidance for Evaluating Vapor Intrusion into Indoor Air Pathways," U.S. EPA, December 2001.
    b. States—The following sixteen states also have regulations or guidance documents regarding vapor intrusion: Alaska, California, Colorado, Connecticut, Indiana, Maine, Massachusetts, Michigan, Minnesota, Nebraska, New Hampshire, New Jersey, New York, Pennsylvania, Washington and Wisconsin.

PART IX: CONTINUING OBLIGATIONS

GGG. What Are "Continuing Obligations"?

1. **Pre-Acquisition "Threshold Criteria":** Each of the three landowner liability protections have threshold criteria that must be met prior to property acquisition, in order for a prospective landowner (buyer or Grantee) to qualify for the protection(s) against CERCLA liability. These are usually called "Threshold Criteria."

   Note: Once again, the three landowner liability protections are generally abbreviated as follows:
   Innocent Landowner—ILO (Also: Innocent Landowner Defense—ILD)
   Contiguous Property Owner—CPO
   Bona Fide Prospective Purchaser—BFPP

2. **Post-Acquisition "Continuing Obligations" Requirements:** Each of the three landowner liability protections also have post-acquisition requirements in order to maintain CERCLA liability. These are usually called "Continuing Obligations."

   Conducting "All Appropriate Inquiries" alone does not provide a landowner with protection against CERCLA liability. The landowner must also comply with all other statutory requirements, including "Continuing Obligations."

3. **Continuing Obligations Always Applicable:** Continuing Obligations apply regardless of when contamination is discovered. It doesn't matter if contamination is discovered during an AAI or after property acquisition.

4. **Synonyms for "Continuing Obligations":** Continuing Obligations can also be referred to as:
   a. "Due Care"—A term which comes from the requirements for the Innocent Landowner Defense, and which generally is associated with affirmative steps that a landowner should take when contamination is encountered and must be responded to (Due Care has established case law);
   b. "Reasonable Steps"—A term which is technically only one component of Continuing Obligations, and which generally is associated with situations where a landowner has already obtained information regarding contamination at the property, e.g., would be more applicable to a BFPP;
   c. "Appropriate Care"—A more general term, and which generally is used in a manner similar to "Reasonable Steps" (although this term is not defined as such by U.S. EPA), i.e., for situations where a landowner has already obtained information regarding contamination (generally BFPPs);
   d. "Long-Term Stewardship"—A broader term that encompasses Continuing Obligations, e.g., institutional and engineering controls, but also includes long-term management of contaminated sites, e.g., life-cycle costs, resources, funding mechanisms, information and data management, etc. (used by U.S. EPA DOE and DOD).

5. **"Common Elements":** Requirements that cut across all the protections are usually called "Common Elements." Common Elements apply to pre- and post-acquisition requirements for all the protections, i.e., "Common Elements" include "Threshold Criteria" as well as "Continuing Obligations."

6. **AAI and Continuing Obligations Are Two Halves of a Whole:** In effect, there are two portions to obtaining and maintaining the "All Appropriate Inquiries" landowner liability protections. The first is conducting an "All Appropriate Inquiry." The second is complying with all Continuing Obligations. Conducting the "All Appropriate Inquiry" is always performed prior to acquisition. Continuing Obligations, generally speaking, apply subsequent to acquisition. (See III: When Do Continuing Obligations and "Additional Appropriate Investigations" Begin?)

7. **New Contamination Can Result in Full CERCLA Liability:** The Continuing Obligations, and its Reasonable Steps provisions, only apply to landowners who do not further contaminate their property:

    "The required reasonable steps relate only to responding to contamination for which the bona fide prospective purchaser, contiguous property owner, or innocent landowner is not responsible. Activities on the property subsequent to purchase that result in new contamination can give rise to full CERCLA liability. That is, more than reasonable steps will likely be required from the landowner if there is new hazardous substance contamination on the landowner's property for which the landowner is liable."
    ("Interim Guidance Regarding Criteria Landowners Must Meet in Order to Qualify for Bona Fide Prospective Purchaser, Contiguous Property Owner, or Innocent Landowner Limitations on CERCLA Liability ('Common Elements')," U.S. EPA, March 6, 2003, pg. 11.
    www.epa.gov/compliance/resources/policies/cleanup/superfund/common-elem-guide.pdf.)

    "(I)f the release is the result of a disposal after the property owner's purchase, then she may be required to undertake full remedial measures as a CERCLA liable party." ("Interim Guidance," Attachment B, pg. 4.)

[Ref: AAI Final Rule, Section II, D, pg. 66072-74.]

HHH. "Continuing Obligation" Requirements

"Continuing Obligations" Requirements For All Protections:
- *Take "Reasonable Steps" with respect to hazardous substances releases, including:*
  - *stop an ongoing or continuing release*
  - *prevent a threatened future release*
  - *prevent or limit human, environmental, or natural resource exposure to any previously released hazardous substance.*
- *Comply with any institutional controls or land use restrictions established or relied on in connection with a response action, including not impeding the effectiveness or integrity of any institutional controls, such as:*
  - *governmental controls (e.g., zoning)*
  - *proprietary controls (e.g., covenants, easements)*
  - *enforcement documents (e.g., orders, consent decrees)*
  - *informational devices (e.g., land record/deed notices).*
- *Provide full cooperation, assistance and access to persons who are authorized to conduct response actions or natural resource restoration at the vessel or facility from which there has been a release or threatened release, including the cooperation and access necessary for the installation, integrity, operation and maintenance of any complete or partial response action or natural resource restoration at the vessel or facility.*
- *Comply with any CERCLA information requests or administrative subpoenas (e.g., Section 104(e) Information Requests).*
- *Provide all legally required notices with respect to the discovery or release of any hazardous substances at the facility. ("Legally required notices" may include those required under federal, state and local laws. Examples of federal notices that may be required include, but are not limited to, those under: CERCLA § 103 (notification requirements regarding released substances); EPCRA § 304 ("emergency notification"); and RCRA § 9002 (notification provisions for underground storage tanks).)*

Note: Regarding the last two items (information requests, notices, etc.), the requirement is somewhat different (but still fundamentally similar) for Innocent Landowners.

Notes Regarding Institutional Controls:

1. Institutional Controls Identified within an AAI: There is no AAI (or ASTM) requirement, within the performance of AAI, to review whether the facility is in compliance with institutional controls or engineering controls. The requirement within AAI is merely to identify the institutional and engineering controls. However, if there are institutional controls at the property, then there is a separate specific requirement to comply with such institutional controls after acquisition, as part of Continuing Obligations, in order to maintain the landowner liability protections.

2. Institutional Controls Discovered or Enforced After Acquisition: The landowner must also comply with land use restrictions and implement institutional controls even if the restrictions/controls were not in place at the time of purchase; or even if restrictions have not been implemented through an enforceable institutional control. For example, in addition to violating restrictions on land use (e.g., applying for a zoning change), a violation could also result if a landowner removed a required notice in the land records, or failed to give required notice to a subsequent purchaser of the property.

III. When Do "Continuing Obligations" (and "Additional Appropriate Investigations") Begin?

1. Broadly speaking, "All Appropriate Inquiries" are done prior to acquisition, while Continuing Obligations begin after property acquisition.

2. With regard to "All Appropriate Inquiries," the dividing line is clear. AAI must be completed prior to property acquisition (transfer of title).

3. With regard to Innocent Landowners and Contiguous Property Owners, because they could not have known of any contamination prior to acquisition, their Continuing Obligations (including Reasonable Steps) begin after acquisition, when contamination is encountered.

4. With regard to Bona Fide Prospective Purchasers, some portions of their Continuing Obligations—particularly Reasonable Steps—can begin earlier if they acquire particular knowledge of contamination prior to acquisition.

5. To some degree, the question of when Reasonable Steps begin for Bona Fide Prospective Purchasers revolves around the question of whether acquiring the necessary data is part of the Reasonable Steps. In other words, if Phase II sampling and analysis would be a prerequisite activity to implementing Reasonable Steps, is then the Phase II sampling and analysis actually part of the Reasonable Steps? If yes, then, particularly for Bona Fide Prospective Purchasers, Reasonable Steps can begin within the "All Appropriate Inquiries."

6. The U.S. EPA concurs:

    "The pre-purchase 'appropriate inquiry' by the bona fide prospective purchaser will most likely inform the bona fide prospective purchaser as to the nature and extent of contamination on the property and what might be considered reasonable steps regarding the contamination—how to stop continuing releases, prevent threatened future releases and prevent or limit human, environmental and natural resource exposures. Knowledge of contamination and the opportunity to plan prior to purchase should be factors in evaluating what are reasonable steps, and could result in greater reasonable steps obligations for a bona fide prospective purchaser." ("Interim Guidance Regarding Criteria Landowners Must Meet in Order to Qualify for Bona Fide Prospective Purchaser, Contiguous Property Owner, or Innocent Landowner Limitations on CERCLA Liability ('Common Elements')," U.S. EPA, March 6, 2003, pg. 11, underlining added. www.epa.gov/compliance/resources/policies/cleanup/superfund/common-elem-guide.pdf.)

7. Separately, the Environmental Professional should provide an opinion within the AAI/Phase I regarding "Additional Appropriate Investigation," if any. Neither the AAI Final Rule nor the ASTM Phase I define when the implementation of those opinions regarding "Additional Appropriate Investigation" should be done. The implementation of any such opinions may be done either before acquisition or subsequent to acquisition.

    While "Additional Appropriate Investigation" can sometimes be Phase II sampling and analysis, they can also be "more of the same" Phase I type activities, e.g., more historical research, government record searches, interviews, site inspections, etc.

8. In the end, it may be left to the judgment of the Environmental Professional and the (prospective) landowner as to whether "Additional Appropriate Investigation" items and/or Phase II sampling and analysis should be done prior to acquisition or whether they may be done post-acquisition.

JJJ. New ASTM "Continuing Obligations" Standard Practice

1. **New Standard Practice:** ASTM Committee E50.02 is developing a Standard Practice for Continuing Obligations (a.k.a. Landowner Appropriate Care of a Contaminated Property). While it will be linked to the Phase I Environmental Site Assessment Standard Practice (E1527-05), the Continuing Obligations Standard Practice will be a self-standing Standard Practice.

2. **Release Date:** The Continuing Obligations Standard Practice will be released by Fall 2006.

3. **Objectives:** The greatest degree of discomfort in the marketplace relates to the uncertainties associated with Continuing Obligations. The underlying objective of the ASTM effort is to bring a measure of certainty to this arena, thereby assisting the affected stakeholders in optimizing the benefits of the landowner liability protections.

4. **Consensus Based:** The development of the Continuing Obligations Standard Practice, as per ASTM policy, includes a consensus-based approach with representation from all affected sectors. Included within the ASTM Committee deliberations are representatives from U.S. EPA.

5. **Continuing Obligations Principles:** The Standard Practice may add clarity, e.g.,
    - "Reasonable Steps" are not intended to constitute remediation,
    - "Reasonable Steps" are not intended to create new obligations,
    - "Reasonable Steps" may be fulfilled through state voluntary cleanup guidance.

6. **Topic Breakdown:** Continuing Obligations may be divided into:
    a. Reasonable Steps,
    b. Institutional and Engineering Controls, and
    c. Legal (i.e., providing cooperation to persons authorized to conduct response actions, complying with information requests, providing legally required notices, etc).

7. **Menu of Available Approaches:** The Standard Practice may provide a menu of available approaches to Continuing Obligations, e.g., Engineering Controls for contaminated soils, Institutional Controls for contaminated groundwater, Vapor Barriers for contaminated vapors.

    As one possible example, if the menu options for Continuing Obligations of contaminated soils can include the use of existing pavement which already covers those soils, this type of clarity would bring a degree of comfort to the regulated industrial and general real estate marketplace.

8. **ASTM May Help Facilitate Use of Institutional Controls:** Institutional Controls (IC) can be particularly effective in proactively addressing Continuing Obligations. The concept of using land use restrictions to promote effective utilization of all real estate is well established, both legally and socially. Proactive implementation of Institutional Controls, with the assistance of Environmental Professionals and legal counsel, and particularly as per the new ASTM Standard Practice on Continuing Obligations of Contaminated Property, will significantly close the "worry gap" regarding Continuing Obligations.

Note: To obtain the new Standard Practice on Continuing Obligations of Contaminated Property when it is released, please contact ASTM: 610-832-9585 or service@astm.org.

KKK. Can "Reasonable Steps" Be Reasonable?

> In acquiring a known contaminated property, prospective landowners likely will be justifiably concerned with the uncertainties associated with Continuing Obligations. For example, there are real concerns that U.S. EPA can easily turn "Reasonable Steps" into large-scale cleanups, in deed if not in word.
>
> There are several proactive possible ways to potentially reduce these concerns. They include:
> a. Utilize the new ASTM "Continuing Obligations Standard Practice" [see also Part JJJ];
> b. Optimize the usage and effectiveness of Institutional and Engineering Controls (particularly in states where statutes have been enacted to facilitate implementation and enforcement of IC/EC, or at least where common law is not a hindrance) [see also Part JJJ.8 and MM.1 and 2]; and
> c. Utilize qualified Environmental Professionals to proactively define the Continuing Obligations within the "All Appropriate Inquiries" prior to acquisition (and not wait until after the AAI has been completed and post-acquisition questions arise) [see also Part KKK.10 and III.6].
> Note: This is not effective in situations where exposure to contaminants cannot be reasonably limited or prevented.

1. **"Reasonable Steps" Are Intended on Being Reasonable:** *"The reasonable steps determination will be a site-specific fact-based inquiry. That inquiry should take into account the different elements of the landowner liability protections and should reflect the balance that Congress sought between protecting certain landowners from CERLCA liability and assuring continued protection of human health and the environment."*
("Interim Guidance Regarding Criteria Landowners Must Meet in Order to Qualify for Bona Fide Prospective Purchaser, Contiguous Property Owner, or Innocent Landowner Limitations on CERCLA Liability ('Common Elements')," U.S. EPA, March 6, 2003, pg. 11-12.
www.epa.gov/compliance/resources/policies/cleanup/superfund/common-elem-guide.pdf.)

2. **"Reasonable Steps" Not Intended as Cleanup:** The intent of Continuing Obligations, and its provision regarding Reasonable Steps, is not to place onerous response and cleanup burdens on persons who are entitled to the landowner liability protections. Instead, the intent is to clarify that all property owners, including those with liability protections, must be responsible environmental stewards, whether in relation to newfound knowledge of releases that should be stopped, threatened releases that should be prevented, or preventing or limiting exposure, etc.

   The U.S. EPA has indicated that, except in unusual circumstances, protected landowners are not expected under the "reasonable steps" provisions to undertake other response actions that would be more properly paid for by the responsible parties who caused the contamination.

   > *"By making the landowner liability protections subject to the obligation to take 'reasonable steps,' EPA believes Congress intended to balance the desire to protect certain landowners from CERCLA liability with the need to ensure the protection of human health and the environment. In requiring reasonable steps from parties qualifying for landowner liability protections, EPA believes Congress did not intend to create, as a general matter, the same types of response obligations that exist for a CERCLA liable party (e.g., removal of contaminated soil, extraction and treatment of contaminated groundwater)."*
   ("Interim Guidance Regarding Criteria Landowners Must Meet in Order to Qualify for Bona Fide Prospective Purchaser, Contiguous Property Owner, or Innocent Landowner Limitations on CERCLA Liability ('Common Elements')," U.S. EPA, March 6, 2003, pg. 9-10.
   www.epa.gov/compliance/resources/policies/cleanup/superfund/common-elem-guide.pdf.)

3. **"Reasonable Steps" Are Site-Specific:** *"What constitutes reasonable steps depends on the facts of each site. For example, reasonable steps may include actions such as removal of drums, securing of the site through fencing and/or other means, appropriate signage warning of the danger, etc. Reasonable steps will be very site-specific . . . At this time, the Agency does not intend to determine or approve reasonable steps at most brownfield sites. It is a concept that will be interpreted in the courts. EPA believes that the existing case law interpreting due care provides a reference point for understanding the requirement to exercise appropriate care by taking reasonable steps."* ("Questions and Answers Regarding Federal Brownfields Property Liability," U.S. EPA, November, 2003, pg. 3.)

4. **Data Gaps Do Not Necessarily Affect AAI Liability Protection:** *"If a person properly conducts all appropriate inquiries pursuant to this rule, including the requirements concerning data gaps at § 312.10, 312.20(g), and 312.21(c)(2), the person may fulfill the all appropriate inquiries requirements of CERCLA sections 107(q), 107(r), and 101(35), even when there are data gaps in the inquiries."* (AAI Final Rule, Section IV, N, pg. 66088-89, underlining added.)

5. **"Reasonable Steps" Are Triggered Despite Data Gaps:** The Final Rule requirements for the landowner liability protections include the following warning regarding Continuing Obligations:

   "Persons claiming to be (bona fide prospective purchasers, contiguous property owners) should keep in mind that failure to identify an environmental condition or identify a release or threatened release of a hazardous substance on, at, in, or to a property during the conduct of all appropriate inquiries does not relieve a landowner from complying with the other post-acquisition statutory requirements for obtaining the liability protection. Landowners must comply with all the statutory requirements to obtain the liability protection. For example, an inability to identify a release or threatened release during the conduct of all appropriate inquiries does not negate the landowner's responsibilities under the statutes to take reasonable steps to stop a release, prevent a threatened release and prevent exposure to any previous release once any release is identified. Complying with the other statutory requirements . . . is not contingent upon the findings of all appropriate inquiries." (AAI Final Rule, Section II, D, pg. 66072-74.)

6. **U.S. EPA May Sometimes Issue Site-Specific "Reasonable Steps" Letters:** *"EPA may, in its discretion, provide a comfort/status letter addressing reasonable steps at a specific site, upon request. EPA anticipates that such letters will be limited to sites with significant federal involvement such that the Agency has sufficient information to form a basis for suggesting reasonable steps (e.g., the site is on the National Priorities List or EPA has conducted or is conducting a removal action on the site). In addition, as the 1997 Comfort/Status Letter Policy provides, '[i]t is not EPA's intent to become involved in typical real estate transactions. . . .'"* ("Interim Guidance," pg. 12.)

7. **Consider Using High Caliber Environmental Professionals:** *"The rigor of the tribal and state-licensed P.E. and P.G. certification processes . . . will ensure that all appropriate inquiries are conducted under the supervision or responsible charge of an individual well qualified to oversee the collection and interpretation of site-specific information and render informed opinions and conclusions regarding the environmental conditions at a property. . . . The Agency's decision to recognize tribal and state-licensed P.E.s and P.G.s reflects the fact that tribal governments and state legislatures hold such professionals responsible (legally and ethically) for safeguarding public safety, public health and the environment."* (AAI Final Rule, Section IV, E, pg. 66079, underlining added.) [See also III.6]

LLL. Examples of "Reasonable Steps"

The following Questions and Answers relating to "Reasonable Steps" are taken verbatim from the U.S. EPA Interim Guidance document on "Common Elements":

Q1: If a person conducts "all appropriate inquiry" with respect to a property where EPA has conducted a removal action, discovers hazardous substance contamination on the property that is unknown to EPA, and then purchases the property, is notification to EPA or the state about the contamination a reasonable step?

A1: Yes. First, bona fide prospective purchasers may have an obligation to provide notice of the discovery or release of a hazardous substance under the legally required notice provision . . .

Q2: Where a property owner discovers unauthorized dumping of hazardous substances on a portion of her property, are site access restrictions reasonable steps?

A2: Site restrictions are likely appropriate as a first step, once the dumping is known to the owner . . .

Q3: If a new property owner discovers some deteriorating fifty-five gallon drums containing unknown material among empty drums in an old warehouse on her property, would segregation of the drums and identification of the material in the drums constitute reasonable steps?

A3: Yes, segregation and identification of potential hazards would likely be appropriate first steps. . . . To the extent the drums have the potential to leak, segregation and containment (e.g., drum overpack) would prevent mishandling and releases to the environment. For storage and handling purposes, an identification of the potential hazards from the material will likely be necessary. Additional identification steps would likely be necessary for subsequent disposal or resale if the material had commercial value.

Q4: If a property owner discovers that the containment system for an on-site waste pile has been breached, do reasonable steps include repairing the breach?

A4: One of the reasonable steps obligations is to "stop any continuing release". . . . In general, the property owner should take actions to prevent contaminant migration where there is a breach from an existing containment system . . .

Q5: If a bona fide prospective purchaser buys property at a Superfund site where part of the approved remedy is an asphalt parking lot cap, but the entity or entities responsible for implementing the remedy . . . are unable to repair the deteriorating cap, . . . should the bona fide prospective purchaser repair the deteriorating asphalt parking lot cap as reasonable steps?

A5: Taking "reasonable steps" includes steps to: "prevent or limit any human, environmental, or natural resource exposure to any previously released hazardous substances". . . . In this instance, the current landowner may be in the best position to identify and quickly take steps to repair the asphalt cap and prevent additional exposures.

Q6: If a property is underlain by contaminated groundwater emanating from a source on a contiguous or adjacent property, do reasonable steps include remediating the groundwater?

A6: Generally not. Absent exceptional circumstances, EPA will not look to a landowner whose property is not a source of a release to conduct groundwater investigations or install groundwater remediation systems . . .

Q7: *If a protected landowner discovers a previously unknown release of a hazardous substance from a source on her property, must she remediate the release?*

A7: *Provided the landowner is not otherwise liable for the release from the source, she should take some affirmative steps to "stop the continuing release," but EPA would not, absent unusual circumstances, look to her for performance of complete remedial measures. However, notice to appropriate governmental officials and containment or other measures to mitigate the release would probably to considered appropriate . . .*

Q8: *If a landowner discovers contamination on her property, does the obligation to take reasonable steps require her to investigate the extent of the contamination?*

A8: *Generally, where the property owner is the first to discover the contamination, she should take certain basic actions to assess the extent of contamination. Absent such an assessment, it will be very difficult to determine what reasonable steps will stop a continuing release, prevent a threatened future release, or prevent or limit exposure. While a full environmental investigation may not be required, doing nothing in the face of a known or suspected environmental hazard would likely be insufficient . . .*

Q9: *If a new purchaser agrees to assume the obligations of a prior owner PRP, as such obligations are defined in an order or consent decree issued or entered into by the prior owner and EPA, will compliance with those obligations satisfy the reasonable steps requirement?*

A9: *Yes . . .*

MMM. <u>Additional Perspective Regarding "Reasonable Steps"—Ronald R. Janke, Jones Day</u>
rrjanke@jonesday.com
Member of ASTM Committee E50 & Subcommittee E50.02

REASONABLE STEPS
Ronald R. Janke, Jones Day

Overview

A landowner must take certain "reasonable steps" to enjoy the defenses accorded to Innocent Landowners, bona fide prospective purchasers, and contiguous property owners against liability for hazardous substances released onto the land pursuant to the 2002 Amendments to the Comprehensive Environmental Response, Compensation and Liability Act of 1980 (CERCLA).[1] This "reasonable steps" requirement is in addition to several other requirements which must be met to establish and preserve these defenses. However, the reasonable steps requirement may prove to be the most difficult of these requirements to understand and achieve.

The Statute

In similar, but not identical terms, CERCLA defines the reasonable steps requirement for these three landowner defenses. The bona fide prospective purchaser defense is available against liability for hazardous substances disposed of at a facility before the person acquired the facility if that person made all appropriate inquiry into the previous ownership and use of the facility before its acquisition. That person must exercise "appropriate care with respect to hazardous substances found at the facility by taking reasonable steps to":

1) "stop any continuing release;"

2) "prevent any threatened future release; and"

3) "prevent or limit human, environmental, or natural resources exposure to any previously released hazardous substances."[2]

The innocent landowner has a defense against CERCLA liability for releases of hazardous substances of which the person did not know or had no reason to know, despite having made all appropriate inquiry, before purchasing the property. The reasonable steps which the innocent landowner must take to avoid liability are defined in the same way as those required of the bona fide properties purchaser.[3] However, the innocent landowner must also exercise due care with respect to the hazardous substances concerned.[4] This additional, and perhaps duplicative requirement, exists because when the innocent landowner defense was established in 1986, it included the requirements of the third-party defense. The 2002 CERCLA Amendments added the reasonable steps requirement but did not change the requirement that the innocent landowner qualify for the third-party defense.

---

[1] 42 USC § § 9601-9675.

[2] 42 USC § 9601(40)(C).

[3] 42 USC § 9601(B)(i)(II).

[4] 42 USC § 9607(b)(3).

The contiguous property owner defense is available to one who owns property which is contaminated by releases of hazardous substances from a contiguous property which he does not own. That person has a defense if, in addition to meeting the other requirements, he "takes reasonable steps to":

1) "stop any continuing releases;"

2) "prevent any threatened future releases; and"

3) "prevent or limit human, environmental, or natural resource exposure to any hazardous substance released from the property owned by that person."[5]

While the statutory texts of the "reasonable steps" element of the three defenses do vary, they are predominately similar and present the same problems of interpretation.

The Reasonable Steps Dilemma

The reasonable steps requirement presents a dilemma for those who would rely upon it: How does one determine what specific acts are required in a particular situation? Of course, courts have the power to ultimately resolve this question, but a court decision is an unsatisfactory answer which comes only after the uncertainty and expense of litigation. While court opinions may eventually provide some guidance, the day when a critical mass of reasonable steps jurisprudence exists is a long way off and the need to determine what acts to take is a current one.

The uncertainty of the reasonable steps requirement can be contrasted with the all appropriate inquiry requirement for the innocent purchaser and bona fide prospective purchase defenses. An understanding of the all appropriate inquiry requirement is guided by an Environmental Protection Agency rule[6] which references a corresponding ASTM standard.[7] Furthermore, determinations under the EPA rule and ASTM standard are guided by an environmental professional whose role both recognize.[8]

EPA's Common Elements Guidance

Early guidance from EPA as to what constitutes reasonable steps may be found in a March 6, 2003 memo issued by the Office of Site Remediation Enforcement, "Interim Guidance Regarding Criteria Landowners Must Meet to Qualify for Bona Fide Prospective Purchases, Contiguous Property Owner or Innocent Landowner Limitations in CERCLA Liability." This memo is known as the "Common Elements" guidance. In their memo EPA interprets the Congressional intent underlying the reasonable steps requirement to be a desire to balance the protection of these landowners from liability with the protection of human health and the environment.

As a general matter, EPA believes that these landowners do not have to take the same types of response actions (excavation of soil or extraction of groundwater) as do liable parties under CERCLA. EPA points to legislation history indicating that absent "exceptional circumstances," reasonable steps would not require groundwater investigations and the installation of remediation systems. On the other hand, EPA indicates that a landowner generally must take some action when contamination is encountered. Citing judicial interpretations of the third-party due care standard, EPA notes that courts have generally required a landowner to take some positive or affirmative action when confronted by hazardous substances on his property.

---

[5] 42 USC § 9607(q).

[6] 40 CFR Part 312, adopted in 70 Federal Register 66070 (November 1, 2005).

[7] ASTM International Standard E1527-05, referenced in 40 CFR § 312.11(a).

[8] 40 CFR § 312.20(a)(2).

EPA correctly states that any reasonable steps determination will be "a site-specific, fact-based inquiry." EPA goes on to give some examples of what would be reasonable steps. In particular, EPA points out that giving timely notification to government authorities of the discovery of contamination and taking basic actions to assess the extent of contamination would be reasonable steps. EPA also states that if a leaking drum is discovered, the drum should be segregated, contained and its contents identified. EPA states that upon request it may, in its discretion, provide a comfort letter addressing reasonable steps at a specific site. If so, EPA may confer with state authorities before issuing such a letter.

EPA All Appropriate Inquiry Rulemaking

In the preamble to the prepared and final All Appropriate Inquiry rules, EPA repeatedly mentions and expands upon an issue which it briefly mentions in the Common Elements guidance. This issue is how imperfect knowledge relates to reasonable care obligations. In the preamble to the proposed All Appropriate Inquiry rule, EPA states: "A person's inability to obtain information regarding a property's ownership or use prior to acquiring a property can affect the landowner's ability to claim a protection from CERCLA liability after acquiring, if a lack of information results in the landowner's inability to comply with any other post-acquisition statutory obligations that are necessary to assert protection from CERCLA liability."[9] As an example, EPA states: "if a person does not identify . . . prior to acquiring a new property, a leaking underground storage tank that exists on the property, the landowner may not have sufficient information . . . to take reasonable steps to stop on-going releases after acquiring the property."[10]

EPA returns to this issue in the preamble to the final All Appropriate Inquiry Rule. The agency states:

> Failure to identify a release or threatened release during the conduct of all appropriate inquiries does not negate the landowner's continuing responsibilities under the statute, including the requirements to take reasonable steps to stop the release, prevent a threatened release, and prevent exposure to the release or threatened release once the landowner has acquired a property. . . .

> The failure to detect a release during the conduct of all appropriate inquiries does not exempt a landowner from his or her post-acquisition Continuing Obligations under other provisions of the statute.[11]

This statement suggests that if a release or threatened release is of the type that a landowner would have to stop or prevent to meet the "reasonable steps" requirement, this action is required even if he is unaware of the release. This interpretation can be questioned. For example, the bona fide prospective purchaser defense refers to the obligation to exercise "appropriate care with respect to hazardous substances found at the facility."[12] If found is read as meaning "discovered," there could be no obligation to take reasonable steps as to hazardous substances which are not "found" by the landowner.

---

[9] 69 Federal Register 52542, 52560 (August 26, 2004).

[10] *Id.*

[11] 70 Federal Register at 66089 (November 1, 2005).

[12] 42 USC § 9601(40)(D).

Other Approaches

ASTM has commenced the development of a standard practice for Continuing Obligations for contaminated property. Also, state Brownfields remediation programs may provide a useful frame of reference. For example, reaching a no further action determination or similar conclusion through a state Brownfields remediation program provides a powerful argument that reasonable steps have been taken with respect to the property conditions addressed, especially if the state program is one endorsed by the EPA.

Whatever approach is taken, developing greater certainty as to what constitutes reasonable steps is critically important if these defenses are going to achieve their intended purpose of encouraging the return of Brownfields to productive use.[13] For Brownfields' redevelopment to be encouraged, reasonable care must become interpreted so that it is understood and potentially applicable as something akin to an attainable safe harbor, rather than as a black hole.

---

[13] This intent is indicated by the official title of the 2002 CERCLA Amendment, which is The Small Business Liability Relief and Brownfields Revitalization Act.

APPENDIX A

U.S. EPA
FINAL RULE FACT SHEET

All Appropriate Inquiries Final Rule

What is "All Appropriate Inquiries"?

"All appropriate inquiries" is the process of evaluating a property's environmental conditions and assessing potential liability for any contamination.

Why is EPA Establishing Standards for Conducting All Appropriate Inquiries?

The 2002 Brownfields Amendments to CERCLA require EPA to promulgate regulations establishing standards and practices for conducting all appropriate inquiries.

Stakeholder Collaboration

A Negotiated Rulemaking Committee consisting of 25 diverse stakeholders developed the proposed rule. Following publication of the proposed rule, EPA provided for a three month public comment period. EPA received over 400 comments from interested parties. Based upon a review and analysis of issues raised by commenters, EPA developed the final rule.

When is the Rule Effective?

The final rule is effective on November 1, 2006—one year after being published in the Federal Register. Until November 1, 2006, both the standards and practices included in the final regulation and the current interim standards established by Congress for all appropriate inquiries (ASTM E1527-00) will satisfy the statutory requirements for the conduct of all appropriate inquiries.

Who is Affected?

The final All Appropriate Inquiries requirements are applicable to any party who may potentially claim protection from CERCLA liability as an innocent landowner, a bona fide prospective purchaser, or a contiguous property owner. Parties who receive grants under the EPA's Brownfields Grant program to assess and characterize properties must comply with the All Appropriate Inquiries standards.

When Must All Appropriate Inquiries be Conducted?

All appropriate inquiries must be conducted or updated within one year of the date of acquisition of a property. If all appropriate inquiries are conducted more than 180 days prior to the acquisition date, certain aspects of the inquiries must be updated.

What Specific Activities Does the Rule Require?

Many of the inquiry's activities must be conducted by, or under the supervision or responsible charge of, an individual who qualifies as an environmental professional as defined in the final rule.

The inquiry of the environmental professional must include:
- interviews with past and present owners, operators and occupants;
- reviews of historical sources of information;
- reviews of federal, state, tribal and local government records;
- visual inspections of the facility and adjoining properties;
- commonly known or reasonably ascertainable information; and
- degree of obviousness of the presence or likely presence of contamination at the property and the ability to detect the contamination.

Additional inquiries that must be conducted by or for the prospective landowner or grantee include:
- searches for environmental cleanup liens;
- assessments of any specialized knowledge or experience of the prospective landowner (or grantee);
- an assessment of the relationship of the purchase price to the fair market value of the property, if the property was not contaminated; and
- commonly known or reasonably ascertainable information.

How Does the Final AAI Rule Differ From the Interim Standard?

The final All Appropriate Inquiries rule does not differ significantly from the ASTM E1527-00 standard. The rule includes all the main activities that previously were performed as part of environmental due diligence such as site reconnaissance, records review, interviews, and documentation of recognized environmental conditions. The final rule, however, enhances the inquiries by extending the scope of a few of the environmental due diligence activities. In addition, the final rule requires that significant data gaps or uncertainties be documented.

Under the final All Appropriate Inquiries rule, interviewing the subject property's current owner or occupants is mandatory. The ASTM E1527-00 standard only required that the environmental professional make a reasonable attempt to conduct such interviews. In addition, the final rule includes provisions for interviewing past owners and occupants of the subject property, if necessary to meet the objectives and performance factors. Under the ASTM E1527-00 standard, the environmental professional had to inquire about past uses of the subject property when interviewing the current property owner.

The final rule also requires an interview with an owner of a neighboring property if the subject property is abandoned. The ASTM E1527-00 standard included such interviews at the environmental professional's discretion.

The final rule does not specify who is responsible for performing record searches, including searches for use limitations and environmental cleanup liens. The ASTM E1527-00 standard specified that these record searches are the responsibility of the user and required that the results be reported to the environmental professional.

Unlike the ASTM E1527-00 standard, the final rule requires the examination of tribal and local government records and more extensive documentation of data gaps.

The final rule includes specific documentation requirements if the subject property cannot be visually inspected. The ASTM E1527-00 standard did not include such requirements.

Who Qualifies as an Environmental Professional?

To ensure the quality of all appropriate inquiries, the final rule includes specific educational and experience requirements for an environmental professional.

The final rule defines an environmental professional as someone who possesses sufficient specific education, training, and experience necessary to exercise professional judgment to develop opinions and conclusions regarding conditions indicative of releases or threatened releases on, at, in, or to a property, sufficient to meet the objectives and performance factors of the rule, and has: (1) a state or tribal issued certification or license and three years of relevant full-time work experience; **or** (2) a Baccalaureate degree or higher in science or engineering and five years of relevant full-time work experience; **or** (3) ten years of relevant full-time work experience.

For more information on the environmental professional definition, please see EPA's Fact Sheet on the Definition of an Environmental Professional.

Will There Be an Updated ASTM Phase I Site Assessment Standard?

Yes. ASTM International updated its E1527-00 standard, "Standard Practice for Environmental Site Assessments: Phase I Environmental Site Assessment Process." EPA establishes that the revised ASTM E1527-05 standard is consistent with the requirements of the final rule for all appropriate inquiries and may be used to comply with the provisions of the rule.

Contact Information

Patricia Overmeyer

U.S. EPA's Office of Brownfields Cleanup and Redevelopment

(202) 566-2774

Overmeyer.Patricia@epa.gov

Also, please see the U.S. EPA's web site at www.epa.gov/brownfields for additional information.

Brownfields Fact Sheet
AAI Final Rule

Solid Waste
and Emergency
Response (5105)

EPA 560-F-05-240
October 2005
www.epa.gov/brownfields/

APPENDIX B

U.S. EPA
AAI DEFINITION OF ENVIRONMENTAL PROFESSIONAL FACT SHEET

All Appropriate Inquiries Rule:
Definition Of Environmental Professional

What Is "All Appropriate Inquiries?"

"All appropriate inquiries" is the process of evaluating a property's environmental conditions and assessing potential liability for any contamination.

Why Is EPA Establishing Standards For Conducting All Appropriate Inquiries?

The 2002 Brownfields Amendments to CERCLA require EPA to develop regulations establishing standards and practices for conducting all appropriate inquiries.

When Is The Rule Effective?

The final rule is effective on November 1, 2006—one year after its publication date in the Federal Register. Until November 1, 2006, both the standards and practices included in the final regulation and the current interim standard established by Congress for all appropriate inquiries (ASTM E1527-00) will satisfy the statutory requirements for the conduct of all appropriate inquiries.

Who Qualifies As An Environmental Professional?

To ensure the quality of all appropriate inquiries, the final rule includes specific educational and experience requirements for an environmental professional. The definition applies only to persons conducting all appropriate inquiries for the specific purposes outlined in the final rule.

The final rule defines an environmental professional as someone who possesses sufficient specific education, training, and experience necessary to exercise professional judgment to develop opinions and conclusions regarding conditions indicative of releases or threatened releases of hazardous substances on, at, in, or to a property, sufficient to meet the objectives and performance factors of the rule. In addition, an environmental professional must have:

- A state or tribal issued certification or license and three years of relevant full-time work experience; or

- A Baccalaureate degree or higher in science or engineering and five years of relevant full-time work experience; or

- Ten years of relevant full-time work experience.

Qualifying As An Environmental Professional Through Certification or License Requirements

Individuals with a state- or tribal-issued license or certification also must have the equivalent of three years full-time relevant experience to qualify as an environmental professional for the purposes of the all appropriate inquiries rule.

The relevant certification and license requirements include and are limited to the following categories:

- A current Professional Engineer's (P.E.) License;

- A current Professional Geologist's (P.G.) License;

- Other current license or certification from a state, tribe, U.S. territory, or the Commonwealth of Puerto Rico to perform environmental site assessments or all appropriate inquiries as defined in the final rule.

Individuals who do not hold one of these licenses or certifications may still qualify as an environmental professional through educational and experience requirements, as explained below.

Qualifying As An Environmental Professional Through Educational Requirements

Individuals who hold a Baccalaureate or higher degree in engineering or science from an accredited institution of higher education and have equivalent of five years full-time relevant experience qualify as an environmental professional under the final rule.

Individuals not meeting the educational requirements may still qualify as an environmental professional through the relevant experience requirements outlined below.

QUALIFYING AS AN ENVIRONMENTAL PROFESSIONAL THROUGH EXPERIENCE REQUIREMENTS

Individuals who do not otherwise meet the qualifications for an environmental professional outlined above may still meet the definition of environmental professional as stated in the final all appropriate inquiries rule if they have the equivalent of ten years of full-time relevant experience.

WHAT IS THE DEFINITION OF RELEVANT EXPERIENCE?

For the purposes of qualifying as an environmental professional under the final rule for all appropriate inquiries, "relevant experience" means:

Participation in the performance of environmental site assessments that may include environmental analyses, investigations, and remediation which involve the understanding of surface and subsurface environmental conditions and the processes used to evaluate these conditions and for which professional judgment was used to develop opinions regarding conditions indicative of releases of hazardous substances.

MAY PERSONS WHO DO NOT QUALIFY AS ENVIRONMENTAL PROFESSIONALS PARTICIPATE IN THE CONDUCT OF ALL APPROPRIATE INQUIRIES?

Individuals who do not meet any of the above requirements may still participate in the conduct of all appropriate inquiries. However, they must work under the supervision or responsible charge of an individual who does meet the requirements for an environmental professional.

HOW DOES THE DEFINITION OF ENVIRONMENTAL PROFESSIONAL IN THE FINAL RULE DIFFER FROM THE ASTM E1527-00 STANDARD ?

Unlike the ASTM E1527-00 standard, the final rule for all appropriate inquiries contains specific certification or licensing, educational, and experience requirements. In addition, the final rule's definition of an environmental professional differs in that it only concerns the qualifications of the individual supervising the conduct of all appropriate inquiries. Individuals without the proper qualifications to meet the definition of an environmental professional may still take part in all appropriate inquiries as long as they are under the supervision or responsible charge of a person who meets those requirements. For example, a person lacking the required certification or license, education, or relevant experience qualifications may perform any of the required activities provided that the environmental professional oversees his or her work.

For a more information on the all appropriate inquiries final rule see EPA's Fact Sheet on the All Appropriate Inquiries Final Rule (EPA 560-F-05-240).

CONTACT INFORMATION

Patricia Overmeyer

U.S. EPA's Office of Brownfields Cleanup and Redevelopment

(202) 566-2774

Overmeyer.Patricia@epa.gov

Also see U.S. EPA's website at ww.epa.gov/brownfields for additional information.

Brownfields Fact Sheet
AAI: Definition of Environmental Professional

Solid Waste
and Emergency
Response (5105)

EPA 560-F-05-241
October 2005
www.epa.gov/brownfields/

APPENDIX C

U.S. EPA
"COMMON ELEMENTS" GUIDANCE REFERENCE SHEET

U.S. Environmental Protection Agency
"COMMON ELEMENTS" GUIDANCE
REFERENCE SHEET

INTRODUCTION

This reference sheet highlights the main points made in EPA's March 6, 2003 guidance entitled *"Interim Guidance Regarding Criteria Landowners Must Meet in Order to Qualify for the Bona Fide Prospective Purchaser, Contiguous Property Owner, or Innocent Landowner Limitations on CERCLA Liability "Common Elements")*, available at:
http://www.epa.gov/compliance/resources/policies/cleanup/superfund/common-elem-guide.pdf

The "Common Elements" are the statutory threshold criteria and ongoing obligations landowners must meet to qualify as a:

- ▶ bona fide prospective purchaser,
- ▶ contiguous property owner, or
- ▶ innocent landowner.

The 2002 Brownfields Amendments to the Superfund law provide conditional <u>CERCLA liability protection</u> to landowners who qualify as bona fide prospective purchasers, contiguous property owners or innocent landowners. For purposes of EPA's "Common Elements" Guidance and this reference sheet, "innocent landowner" refers only to unknowing purchasers as defined in CERCLA § 101(35)(A)(i).

Who are Bona Fide Prospective Purchasers (BFPPs)?

- ▶ Persons who meet the CERCLA § 101(40) criteria and the CERCLA § 107(r) criteria.
- ▶ Purchasers who buy property <u>after</u> January 11, 2002.
- ▶ BFPPs must perform all appropriate inquiry prior to purchase and may buy *knowing, or having reason to know*, of contamination on the property.

Who are Contiguous Property Owners (CPOs)?

- ▶ Persons who meet the CERCLA § 107(q)(1)(A) criteria.
- ▶ Owners of property that is *not* the source of the contamination. Such property is "contiguous" to, or otherwise similarly situated to, a facility that is the source of contamination found on their property.
- ▶ CPOs must perform all appropriate inquiry prior to purchase and buy *without*

1

knowing, or having reason to know, of contamination on the property.

Who are Innocent Landowners (ILOs)?

- ▶ Persons who meet the CERCLA § 107(b)(3) criteria (including due care) and the CERCLA § 101(35) criteria.
- ▶ ILO's must perform all appropriate inquiry prior to purchase and must buy *without knowing, or having reason to know*, of contamination on the property.

THE COMMON ELEMENTS

A person asserting BFPP, CPO or ILO status has to prove that it meets the applicable criteria.

THRESHOLD CRITERIA

To qualify as a BFPP, CPO, or ILO, a person must perform "all appropriate inquiry" before buying the property.

BFPPs and CPOs must *also* demonstrate that they are not potentially liable nor "affiliated" with any other person who is potentially liable for response costs at the property.

All Appropriate Inquiry
BFPPs, CPOs, and ILOs must perform "all appropriate inquiry" into the previous ownership and uses of property before buying the property.

> **Common Elements**
> **of the Brownfields Amendments**
> **Landowner Provisions**
>
> *Threshold Criteria:*
> ▶ all appropriate inquiry
> ▶ no affiliation with a liable party
>
> *Continuing Obligations:*
> ▶ compliance with land use restrictions and institutional controls
> ▶ taking reasonable steps with respect to hazardous substances on property
> ▶ cooperation, assistance and access
> ▶ compliance with information requests and administrative subpoenas
> ▶ providing legally required notices

BFPPs may buy property with knowledge of contamination and maintain their protection from liability. The CPO and ILO liability protections, in contrast, do *not* apply if the purchaser knew, or had reason to know, of contamination prior to purchase.

EPA will publish regulations and guidance on the all appropriate inquiry standard in the future. For property purchased before May 1997, statutory factors are to be applied. CERCLA § 101(35)(B)(iv)(I). For property purchased after May 1997 and until EPA promulgates a regulation establishing the all appropriate inquiry standard, an ASTM Phase I report may satisfy the standard. CERCLA § 101(35)(B)(iv)(II). EPA is to promulgate a regulation establishing the all appropriate inquiry standard by 2004. CERCLA § 101(35)(B)(ii), (iii).

Affiliation

BFPPs or CPOs must not be potentially liable or affiliated with any other person who is potentially liable for the site response costs. "Affiliated with" includes direct and indirect familial relationships and many contractual, corporate, and financial relationships.

ILOs cannot have a contractual relationship with a liable party.

CONTINUING OBLIGATIONS CRITERIA

To maintain liability protection, landowners must meet the following continuing obligations during their property ownership.

Compliance with Land Use Restrictions and Institutional Controls
BFPPs, CPOs and ILO's must:

> ▶ be in compliance with any land use restrictions established or relied on in connection with the response action;
> ▶ not impede the effectiveness or integrity of any institutional control employed in connection with a response action.

EPA believes the Brownfields Amendments require BFPPs, CPOs and ILOs to:

> ▶ comply with land use restrictions and implement institutional controls even if the restrictions/controls were not in place at the time of purchase; and
> ▶ comply with land use restrictions relied on in connection with the response action even if restrictions haven't been implemented through an enforceable institutional control.

Reasonable Steps
BFPPs, CPOs and ILO's are required to take reasonable steps to:

> ▶ Stop continuing releases;
> ▶ Prevent threatened future releases; and
> ▶ Prevent or limit human, environmental, or natural resource exposure to earlier hazardous substance releases.

The reasonable steps requirement balances Congress' objectives of protecting certain landowners from CERCLA liability, and protecting human health and the environment.

As a general matter, EPA does not believe Congress intended BFPPs, CPOs and ILOs to have the same types of response obligations that CERCLA liable parties have (e.g., removal of contaminated soil, extraction and treatment of contaminated groundwater). The required reasonable steps relate only to responding to contamination for which the BFPP, CPO, or ILO is *not responsible*. Activities on the property after purchase resulting in *new contamination* can give rise to full CERCLA liability. *See* Attachment B to EPA's guidance for more on reasonable steps in a "question and answer" format.

EPA may provide a comfort/status letter suggesting reasonable steps at a specific site. EPA intends to limit these letters to sites where EPA has sufficient information to form a basis for suggesting reasonable steps (e.g., the site is on the National Priorities List or EPA has conducted or is conducting a removal action on the site). Providing such a letter is a matter of Regional discretion. *See* Attachment C to EPA's guidance for a sample "reasonable steps" comfort/status letter.

Cooperation, Assistance, and Access
BFPPs, CPOs and ILOs must provide full cooperation, assistance, and access to persons authorized to conduct response actions or natural resource restoration, including the cooperation and access necessary for the installation, integrity, operation, and maintenance of any complete or partial response action or natural resource restoration.

Compliance with Information Requests and Administrative Subpoenas
BFPPs and CPOs must comply with CERCLA information requests and administrative subpoenas.

Provision of Legally Required Notices
BFPPs and CPOs must provide legally required notices related to the discovery or release of hazardous substances at the facility.

"Legally required notices" may include those required under federal, state, and local laws. Examples of federal notice requirements include: CERCLA § 103 (notification requirements regarding released substances); EPCRA § 304 ("emergency notification"); and RCRA § 9002 (underground storage tanks notification provisions).

Summary: Common Element among the Brownfields Amendments Landowner Provisions	Bona Fide Prospective Purchaser	Contiguous Property Owner	Section 101 (35)(A)(i) Innocent Landowner
All appropriate inquiry	✔	✔	✔
No affiliation demonstration	✔	✔	*
Compliance with land use restrictions and institutional controls	✔	✔	✔
Taking reasonable steps	✔	✔	✔
Cooperation, assistance, access	✔	✔	✔
Compliance with information requests and administrative subpoenas	✔	✔	**
Providing legally required notices	✔	✔	***

* Although the innocent landowner provision does not contain this "affiliation" language, in order to meet the statutory criteria of the innocent landowner liability protection, a person must establish by a preponderance of the evidence that the act or omission that caused the release or threat of release of hazardous substances and the resulting damages were caused by a third party with whom the person does not have an employment, agency, or contractual relationship. CERCLA § 107(b)(3). Contractual relationship is defined in section 101(35)(A).

** Compliance with information requests and administrative subpoenas is not specified as a statutory criterion for achieving and maintaining the section 101(35)(A)(i) innocent landowner liability protection. However, CERCLA requires compliance with administrative subpoenas from all persons, and timely, accurate, and complete responses from all recipients of EPA information requests.

*** Provision of legally required notices is not specified as a statutory criterion for achieving and maintaining the section 101(35)(A)(i) innocent landowner liability protection. These landowners may, however, have independent notice obligations under federal, state and local laws.

QUESTIONS

Questions regarding this reference sheet or EPA's Common Elements Guidance should be directed to Cate Tierney in OSRE's Regional Support Division (202-564-4254, Tierney.Cate@EPA.gov), Greg Madden in OSRE's Policy & Program Evaluation Division (202-564-4229, Madden.Gregory@EPA.gov) or to the Landowner Liability Protection Subgroup contacts listed by Region below.

Landowner Liability Protection Subgroup Regional Contacts

Region	Contact	Phone
Region 1:	Joanna Jerison	617-918-1781
Region 2:	Michael Mintzer	212-637-3168
	Paul Simon	212-637-3152
Region 3:	Joe Donovan	215-814-2483
	Leo Mullin	215-814-3172
	Heather Gray Torres	215-814-2696
Region 4:	Kathleen Wright	404-562-9574
Region 5:	Peter Felitti	312-886-5114
	Thomas Krueger	312-886-0562
	Larry Kyte	312-886-4245
Region 6:	Mark Peycke	214-665-2135
Region 7:	Denise Roberts	913-551-7559
Region 8:	Suzanne Bohan	303-312-6925
	Matthew Cohn	303-312-6853
	Nancy Mangone	303-312-6903
Region 9:	Bill Keener	415-972-3940
Region 10:	Cyndy Mackey	206-553-2569

APPENDIX D

U.S. EPA
COMPARISONS BETWEEN AAI AND ASTM E1527-00

Comparison of the Final All Appropriate Inquiries Standard and the ASTM E1527-00 Environmental Site Assessment Standard

INTRODUCTION

On January 11, 2002, President Bush signed into law the Small Business Liability Relief and Brownfields Revitalization Act (the Brownfields Amendments), which amended the Comprehensive Environmental Response, Compensation and Liability Act (CERCLA), 42 U.S.C. § 9601 et seq. The Brownfields Amendments require the Environmental Protection Agency (EPA) to develop regulations establishing federal standards and practices for conducting all appropriate inquiries. Congress included in the Brownfields Amendments a list of criteria that the Agency must address in the regulations (section 101(35)(B)(iii) of CERCLA).

Subtitle B of Title II of the Brownfields Amendments revised the liability provisions of CERCLA Section 101(35) by clarifying the requirements necessary to establish the innocent landowner defense under CERCLA. In addition, the Brownfields Amendments amended CERCLA by providing additional liability protections for contiguous property owners and bona fide prospective purchasers. For the first time since the enactment of CERCLA in 1980, a person may purchase property with the knowledge that the property is contaminated without being held potentially liable for the cleanup of the contamination. To claim protection from liability, a prospective property owner must comply with the statutory requirements for obtaining the contiguous property owner or bona fide prospective purchaser liability defenses. Among these is the requirement to, prior to the date of acquisition of the property, undertake "all appropriate inquiries" into prior ownership and uses of a property.

The all appropriate inquiries requirements are applicable to any public or private party who may potentially claim protection from CERCLA liability as an innocent landowner, a bona fide prospective purchaser, or a contiguous property owner. In addition, parties receiving grants to conduct characterizations or assessments of brownfields properties under EPA's Brownfields Grant program must conduct the property characterization and assessment in compliance with the all appropriate inquiries requirements.

The purpose of this document is to present a comparison of the all appropriate inquiries requirements included in the final federal regulations and the requirements of the interim standard, the ASTM E1527-00 standard for Phase I environmental site assessments. The ASTM E1527-00 standard is the most prevalent industry standard for conducting Phase I environmental site assessments. This document highlights the main differences between the requirements of the final regulation and the ASTM E1527-00 standard for Phase I environmental site assessments.

Please note that in conjunction with the development of EPA's final rule setting federal standards for the conduct of all appropriate inquiries, ASTM International updated its E1527-00 standard. The new ASTM E1527-05 Phase I Environmental Site Assessment Standard is consistent and compliant with EPA's final rule and may be used to comply with the provisions of the all appropriate inquiries final rule. The differences outlined below apply only to the ASTM E1527-00 standard and are provided to assist the regulatory community in understanding the incremental differences between the requirements of the final rule and the previous ASTM

Comparison of the Final All Appropriate
Inquiries Standard and the ASTM E1527-00
Environmental Site Assessment Standard

1

EPA-560-F-05-242
October 2005
www.epa.gov/brownfields/

E1527 standard, which was the interim standard designated by the Brownfields Law. The differences discussed below are not applicable to the newly revised ASTM E1527-05 standard.

CROSSWALK LINKING THE FINAL AAI STANDARD AND THE ASTM E1527-00

To facilitate comparison between the two standards, Exhibit 1 presents a crosswalk linking the sections of all appropriate inquiries final rule with the relevant or corresponding sections of the ASTM E1527-00 standard, the interim standard that will remain in place until the effective date of the final rule. The first column in Exhibit 1 provides a list of the major activities required by the final rule. The second column in Exhibit 1 provides citations to the applicable sections of the regulation where the requirements are discussed. The third column in Exhibit 1 presents the corresponding sections of the ASTM E1527-00 standard. The fourth column in Exhibit 1 provides references to corresponding sections of the revised ASTM standard, ASTM E1527-05.

COMPARISON OF THE FINAL AAI STANDARD AND THE ASTM E1527-00 STANDARD

The final rule setting federal standards for conducting all appropriate inquiries includes requirements that correspond to all the major activities that are currently performed as part of environmental due diligence under the ASTM E1527-00 standard, such as site reconnaissance, record review, interviews, and documentation of environmental conditions. The final rule, however, enhances the inquiries by extending the scope of some of the environmental due diligence activities. In addition, the final rule establishes a more stringent definition of an environmental professional than the ASTM E1527-00 standard. The key differences between the two standards are summarized in Exhibit 2.

Each of the activities presented in Exhibit 2 is addressed in more depth in the sections following Exhibit 2.

EPA-560-F-05-242
October 2005
www.epa.gov/brownfields/

2

*Comparison of the Final All Appropriate
Inquiries Standard and the ASTM E1527-00
Environmental Site Assessment Standard*

Exhibit 1: Crosswalk between the All Appropriate Inquiries Rule and the ASTM E1527-00 Standard

Definitions and Requirements	Final AAI Standard[1]	ASTM E1527-00	ASTM E1527-05
Purpose	312.1(a)	1.1	1.1, 6.7
Applicability	312.1(b)	4.1, 4.2	4.1, 4.2, 4.5.3
Scope	312.1(c)	1	1
Disclosure Obligations	312.1(d)	Not specified	Not specified
Definition of Abandoned Property	312.10	Not defined	3.2.1
Definition of Adjoining Properties	312.10	3.3.2	3.2.4
Definition of Data Gap	312.10	Not defined	3.2.20
Definition of Environmental Professional	312.10	3.3.12	3.2.29; Appendix X2
Definition of Relevant Experience	312.10	Not defined	Appendix X2
Definition of Good Faith	312.10	Not defined	3.2.35
Definition of Institutional Controls	312.10	3.2.17	3.2.42
References	312.11	2	2
List of Components in All Appropriate Inquiries	312.20(a)	6	6, 7
Shelf Life of the Written Report	312.20(a)-(b)	4.6, 4.7	4.6, 4.7
Reports Prepared for Third Parties	312.20(c)-(d)	4.7	4.7
Objectives	312.20(e)	6.1	7.1
Contaminants of Concern	312.20(e)	1.1	1.1
Performance Factors	312.20(f)	7.1	8.1
Data Gaps	312.20(g)	7.3.2	12.7
Interview with Current and Past Owners and Occupants of the Subject Property	312.23(b), 312.23(c)	9	10
Interview with Neighboring or Nearby Property Owners or Occupants in the Case of Inquiries Conducted at Abandoned Properties	312.23(d)	Not specified	10.5.5
Review of Historical Sources: Suggested Sources	312.24(a)	7.3.4	8.3.4
Review of Historical Sources: Period to Be Covered	312.24(b)	7.3.2	8.3.2
Searches for Recorded Cleanup Liens	312.25	5.2, 7.3.4.4	6.2, 6.4, 8.3.4.4, 10.8.1.10
Records of Activity and Use Limitations (e.g., Engineering and Institutional Controls)	312.26	5.2	8.3.4.4
Government Records Review: List of Records	312.26(a), 312.26(b)	7.2	8.2
Government Records Review: Search Distance	312.26(c), 312.26(d)	7.1.2, 7.2	8.1.2
Site Visit: Requirements	312.27(a), 312.27(b)	8	9
Site Visit: Limitations	312.27(c)	8.2.4	9.2.4, 9.4
Specialized Knowledge or Experience	312.28	5.3	6.3, 12.3
The Relationship of the Purchase Price to the Value of the Property	312.29	5.4	6.5
Commonly Known or Reasonably Ascertainable Information about the Property	312.30	7.1.4	4.1, 6.6,
The Degree of Obviousness of the Presence or Likely Presence of Contamination	312.31	11.6, 11.7	12.6, 12.8, X.3
Signed Declarations to Be Included in the Written Report	312.21(d)	11.7, 11.11	12.12, 12.13

---

[1] Citations in column 2 are to Title 40 of the Code of Federal Regulations (e.g. 40 C.F.R. § 312.20).

Comparison of the Final All Appropriate Inquiries Standard and the ASTM E1527-00 Environmental Site Assessment Standard

3

EPA-560-F-05-242
October 2005
www.epa.gov/brownfields/

Exhibit 2: Summary of Main Differences between the Final All Appropriate Inquiries Regulation and the ASTM E1527-00 Standard

Main Differences	Final AAI Standard	ASTM E1527-00
Definition of Environmental Professional	• Specific certification/license, education, and experience requirements • Applies only to individuals supervising all appropriate inquiries	• No specific certification, licensing, education, or experience requirements • Applies to all individuals involved in conducting all appropriate inquiries
Interview with Current Owner and Occupants of the Subject Property	Mandatory	A reasonable attempt must be made to interview key site manager and reasonable number of occupants
Interview with Past Owner and Occupants	Interviews with past owners and occupants must be conducted as necessary to achieve the objectives and performance factors in §§ 312.20(e)-(f)	Not required, but must inquire about past uses of the subject property when interviewing current owner and occupants
Interview with Neighboring or Nearby Property Owners or Occupants	Mandatory at abandoned properties	Discretionary
Review of Historical Sources: period to be covered	From the present back to when the property first contained structures or was used for residential, agricultural, commercial, industrial or governmental purposes	All obvious uses from the present back to the property's first obvious developed use or 1940, whichever is earlier
Records of Activity and Use Limitations (e.g., Engineering and Institutional Controls) and Environmental Cleanup Liens	• No requirement as to who is responsible for the search • Scope of environmental cleanup lien search includes those liens filed or recorded under federal, state, tribal or local law	• User's responsibility • The search results must be reported to the environmental professional • Scope of environmental cleanup lien search is limited to reasonably ascertainable land title records
Government Records Review	• Federal, state, tribal, and local • Records	• Federal and state records • Local records/sources at the discretion of the environmental professional
Site Inspection	• Visual inspection of subject property and adjoining properties required • Limited exemption with specific requirements if the subject • property cannot be visually inspected	• Visual inspection of subject property required. No exemption. • No specific requirement to inspect adjoining properties; only to report anything actually observed
Contaminants of Concern	<u>Parties seeking CERCLA defense:</u> • CERCLA hazardous substances <u>EPA Brownfields Grant recipients:</u> • CERCLA hazardous substances, pollutants or contaminants • petroleum/petroleum products • controlled substances	CERCLA hazardous substances and petroleum products
Data Gaps	• Requires identification of sources consulted to address data gaps and comments on significance of data gap with regard to the ability of the environmental professional to identify conditions indicative of releases and threatened releases	• Generally discretionary; • Sources that revealed no findings must be documented.
Shelf Life of the Written Report	• One year, with some updates required after 180 days	• Updates of specific activities recommended after 180 days

APPENDIX E

HOW TO OBTAIN RELEVANT DOCUMENTS

How to Obtain Relevant Documents

- **Small Business Liability Relief and Brownfields Revitalization Act:**
  ("The Brownfields Amendments" H.R. 2869)
  www.epa.gov/brownfields/html-doc/hr2869.htm

- **U.S. EPA AAI Final Rule (Federal Register):**
  www.epa.gov/brownfields/aai/aai_final_rule.pdf
  www.epa.gov/swerosps/bf/aai/aai_final_rule.pdf

- **ASTM Phase I Standard Practice (E1527-05):**
  ASTM 610-832-9585 or service@astm.org

- **Continuing Obligations:**
  "Interim Guidance Regarding Criteria Landowners Must Meet in Order to Qualify for Bona Fide Prospective Purchaser, Contiguous Property Owner, or Innocent Landowner Limitations on CERCLA Liability ('Common Elements')," U.S. EPA, March 6, 2003.
  www.epa.gov/compliance/resources/policies/cleanup/superfund/common-elem-guide.pdf

- **AAI Final Rule Fact Sheet:**
  (EPA Publication 560-F-05-240, November 2005)
  www.epa.gov/brownfields/aai/aai_final_factsheet.pdf

- **AAI Definition of Environmental Professional Fact Sheet:**
  (EPA Publication 560-F-05-2401)
  www.epa.gov/brownfields/aai/ep-deffactsheet.pdf

- **Comparison of Final Rule to Interim Standard (ASTM E1527-00):**
  (EPA Publication 560-F-05-242, November 2005)
  www.epa.gov/brownfields/aai/compare_astm.pdf

- **Other U.S. EPA Brownfields AAI Documents:**
  www.epa.gov/brownfields/regneg.htm

- **Other U.S. EPA Brownfields Information:**
  www.epa.gov/brownfields

- **Other U.S. EPA General Information:**
  www.epa.gov
  www.epa.gov/fedrgstr

APPENDIX F

**CREDENTIALS
OF
BARRY A. CIK**

Credentials

BARRY A. CIK, BCEE, PE, CP, QEP, CHMM, REM
Chief Engineer, G.E.M. Testing & Engineering Labs, Cleveland, Ohio
216-781-4120; 216-381-3153; 216-288-0995; or barry@gemtesting.com

---

A quarter century of experience investigating and assessing hazardous materials/contamination, resolving environmental problems and protecting human health, safety and the environment

---

Expertise:

- Environmental and Geo-Environmental Assessments including EPA "All Appropriate Inquiry"
- Hazardous and Toxic Substances Evaluations • Forensic Environmental Investigations
- Remediation Analysis, Design & Project Management
- Author, *"Commercial Landowner CERCLA Liability Protection: Understanding the Final EPA 'All Appropriate Inquiries' Rule and Revised ASTM Phase I,"* Government Institutes, 2006.

Credentials:

B.S. Civil Engineering, 1978, *Ohio State University*
  Environmental and Engineering Surveys

C.E. Civil Engineering Advanced Professional Degree
  1981, *Ohio State University*
  Environmental & Engineering Surveys & Materials

Registered Professional Engineer—PE [#47615]
  State of Ohio Engineers Board of Registration

Certified Professional—CP [#109]
  State of Ohio EPA VAP

Certified Hazardous Materials Manager
  Master Level—CHMM [#10795]
  Institute of Hazardous Materials Management

Board Certified Environmental Engineer [#98-20076]
  Diplomate Environmental Engineer—BCEE/DEE
  Hazardous Waste Management Specialization
  American Academy of Environmental Engineers

Qualified Environmental Professional QEP [#01960005]
  Institute of Professional Environmental Practice

Registered Environmental Manager—REM [#05594]
  National Registry of Environmental Professionals

Certified Diplomate Forensic Engineer [#681]
  National Academy of Forensic Engineers

Environmental Professional
  U.S. EPA "All Appropriate Inquiries" Final Rule

Note: The above credentials, licenses and certifications are listed for identification purposes only.
No implication is intended that these credentialing entities endorse or approve this presentation.

Client Experience:

- Resolved environmental concerns and minimized environmental risks for over three thousand clients including *lenders, attorneys, chemical and manufacturing industries, distribution facilities, commercial businesses, real estate investors, developers, schools, multifamily structures and government entities.*

- Protected clients against potential accusations of negligence, assisted in due care and litigation situations including expert witness testimony and enhanced overall client security.

- Interacted/consulted with the majority of the larger banks, including trust departments, in the State of Ohio, as well as with nearly one thousand attorneys.

- Provided technical analysis and representation on behalf of clients to the Ohio EPA, Ohio Bureau of Underground Storage Tanks, Fannie Mae, Freddie Mac and other governmental agencies.

Public Service (Past and/or Present):

- Co-authored "Manual and Laboratory Exercises for Remote Sensing of the Environment." Mintzer, Olin, W.; Ray, John R.; and Cik, Barry A., 1983. Burgess Publishing Co., Alpha Editions (Official text within Civil Engineering Department at Ohio State University as well as at Wright State University)

- Featured speaker on various environmental topics for Ohio Society of Professional Engineers, Construction Specifications Institute, Cuyahoga County Planning Commission, National Business Institute, Ohio Building Environment Council and various law firms

- Featured guest articles in Environmental Law Journal of Ohio, Medical Digest, Acquisition Magazine, Ohio Building Environment Report, Ohio Engineer, Appraisal Institute and Ohio Law Magazine

- Former President/Committee Chairman for local chapters of several professional societies

- Memberships/affiliations with various environmental engineering & socially conscious associations

Offices Held in Professional Organizations (Past and/or Present):

President, Ohio Society of Professional Engineers, Cleveland East Chapter
Chairman, American Society of Civil Engineers, Cleveland Chapter, Environmental Committee
Chairman, American Society of Civil Engineers, Cleveland Chapter, Geotechnical Committee
Trustee, Cleveland Society of Professional Engineers
Trustee, Building Environment Council

Professional Standards Development (Past and/or Present):

ASTM E50	Environmental Assessment, Risk Management & Corrective Action Committee Including E50.02 Environmental Site Assessments and E50.06 Forensic Environmental Investigations
ASTM E51	Lender Secured Creditor Committee
ASTM D18	Soils & Rock Committee
ASTM E27	Hazard Potential of Chemicals Committee
ASTM F15	Consumer Products Committee

Affiliations (Past and/or Present):

National Society of Professional Engineers
American Society of Civil Engineers
Amer. Society Photogrammetry Remote Sensing
ASTM Standards Committees (Various)
Academy Certified Hazardous Materials Managers
Air and Waste Management Association
National Academy Forensic Engineers Sr. Member
Association of Independent Scientific, Engineering
   & Testing Firms (ACIL)
Professional Firms Practicing in the
   Geosciences (ASFE)
Building Environment Council of Ohio
Institute of Professional Environmental Practice

Union of Concerned Scientists
Environmental Health Watch
Ohio Environmental Council
Soil & Water Conservation Society
The Nature Conservancy
Environmental Defense
Natural Resources Defense Council
HEAL (Human Ecology Action League)
American Bankers Association Service Member
Ohio & Cleveland Mortgage Bankers Associations
Association for Commercial Real Estate (NAIOP)
International Association of Corporate Real Estate
   Executives (NACORE)